# JACK HANNA'S
# AWESOME
# ANIMAL
# ALMANAC

## Hello, I'm Jack Hanna!

**IT'S MY JOB** to know a lot about animals, and I decided to share what I've learned over the years in this Animal Almanac. I'm the Director Emeritus of the Columbus Zoo and Aquarium and the host of two TV shows: *Jack Hanna's Into the Wild* and *Jack Hanna's Wild Countdown*, so I've spent most of my life surrounded by wildlife.

This book is 192 pages long and contains fun facts about more than 230 animals! But that's not even close to the number of animals that exist on Earth. There are 7.77 million different species on the planet—and we've only described 12 percent of them! Writing something about all of them would take a much, much longer book. So instead, I've put together a guide to some of my favorites, organized by some of the categories that make them unique. I hope this book teaches you more about the awesome animals that inhabit our world and makes you want to discover even more!

Above you can see me hanging out with a zebra I met in South Africa while filming *Jack Hanna's Into the Wild* in 2010. On the right is a photo my wife Suzi took of me with a mountain goat in Glacier National Park!

# Table of Contents

What is an Animal?   6

Vertebrates vs. Invertebrates   7

Animal Groups   8

History of Life   10

Arctic   12

Bipedal   18

Camouflage   24

Domesticated   30

Endangered   36

Flight   42

Group Living   48

Hooves   54

Insects   60

Jaws   66

Kooky   72

Lazy   78

Migration   84

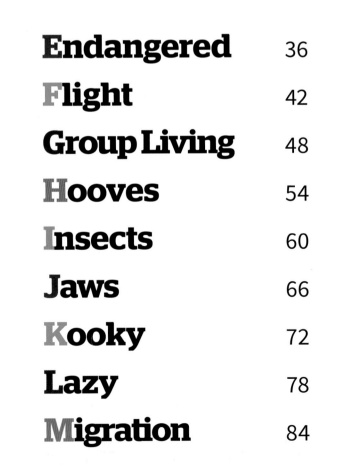

| | |
|---|---|
| **N**octurnal | 90 |
| **O**mnivorous | 96 |
| **P**redators | 102 |
| **Q**uick | 108 |
| **R**odents | 114 |
| **S**pots | 120 |

| | |
|---|---|
| **T**entacles | 126 |
| **U**rsine | 132 |
| **V**enomous | 138 |
| **W**eb-Footed | 144 |
| **X**erophilous | 150 |
| **Y**appy | 156 |
| **Z**ombies | 162 |
| **I**ndex | 168 |

# What's an Animal?

**AN ANIMAL** is a living organism that can breathe. Animals can move—even if just a little bit—and have senses. They can also eat and reproduce! Some are more complex than others, and they come in a variety of shapes and sizes. For example, coral seems a lot like a plant, but it's technically an animal!

One of the big differences between plants and animals is actually microscopic! If you looked at plant and animal cells under a microscope, you would see that plant cells have walls and animal cells don't.

Plants make their own food using photosynthesis, while animals depend on plants and other animals for food. Plants also don't have the ability to see, and don't have the complex nervous system animals do.

# Vertebrates vs. Invertebrates

**SCIENTISTS DIVIDE** animals into two main groups: invertebrates and vertebrates. Vertebrates have backbones or spines, and invertebrates don't.

VERTEBRATES ARE OFTEN BIGGER THAN INVERTEBRATES, BECAUSE THEY HAVE A BONE STRUCTURE TO HELP SUPPORT THEIR BODIES. THERE ARE ABOUT 57,000 DIFFERENT SPECIES OF VERTEBRATES!

EVEN THOUGH THEY TEND TO BE SMALL INDIVIDUALLY, INVERTEBRATES MAKE UP 98 PERCENT OF THE ANIMAL KINGDOM! THERE ARE AT LEAST 2 MILLION DIFFERENT SPECIES OF INVERTEBRATES.

# Animal Groups

**BEYOND VERTEBRATES AND INVERTEBRATES,** animals are categorized into more specific groups. If certain vertebrates share characteristics like feathers and wings, for example, they will be put into the same group.

## Mammals

**MAMMALS ARE WARM-BLOODED** and have hair or fur. They generally birth live young and feed them with milk—the egg-laying platypus and echidna are exceptions to this rule!

WARM-BLOODED ANIMALS CAN CONTROL THEIR OWN BODY TEMPERATURE (LIKE WE DO!) WHILE COLD-BLOODED ANIMALS RELY ON THEIR ENVIRONMENT AND THE SUN TO REGULATE THEIR BODY TEMPERATURE.

## Birds

**BIRDS ARE WARM-BLOODED** animals that lay eggs and have feathers. Most birds can fly, but not all can. Some exceptions include the ostrich, penguin and cassowary.

## Reptiles

**REPTILES ARE SCALY,** cold-blooded creatures that usually lay eggs. Unlike fish, which also have scales, reptiles have lungs and most often live on land!

## Amphibians

**BORN IN THE WATER,** amphibians first develop gills before transitioning to lungs. These animals have the unique ability of being able to live on land and in water!

## Arthropods →

**CHARACTERIZED BY THEIR** segmented bodies and tough exoskeletons, the arthropod group includes both insects and crustaceans.

## Echinoderms

**MOVING VERY SLOWLY** through the sea, echinoderms have a skeleton, even if it's a very loose version of one. Although you might not see them swimming like a fish, sea stars and sea cucumbers do swim!

## Worms →

**WITH SOFT,** usually tubular bodies, worms inhabit both the ocean and land. Sometimes, they even live in other animals as parasites!

## Mollusks

**WITH NO BACKBONE** to worry about, mollusks have squishy, soft bodies. Often mollusks have hard shells to protect themselves—a snail is a good example!

## Sponges →

**ALTHOUGH THEY DON'T** have brains, eyes or mouths, sponges are considered animals! They do swim when they're young, before attaching themselves to the sea floor, and feed by filtering food into their bodies.

## Coelenterates

**WHAT SETS THE** coelenterate apart from the sponge is that it has a mouth! Some coelenterates, like the jellyfish and sea anemone, even have tentacles.

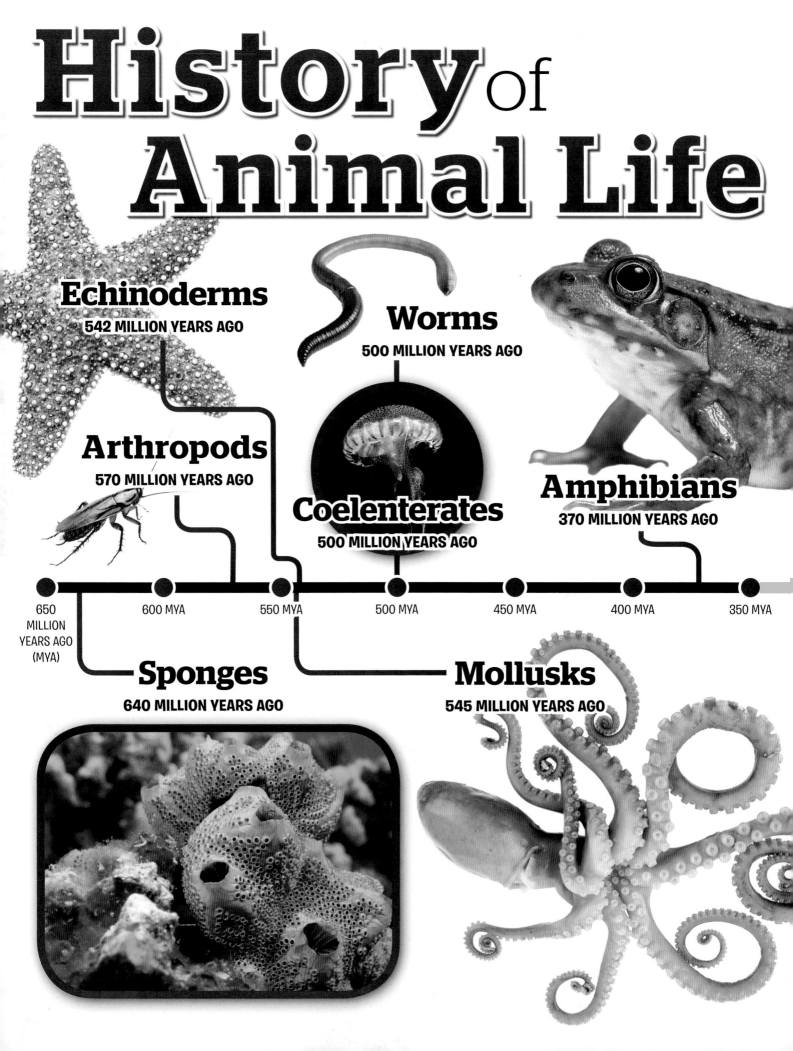

# History of Animal Life

**Echinoderms**
542 MILLION YEARS AGO

**Worms**
500 MILLION YEARS AGO

**Arthropods**
570 MILLION YEARS AGO

**Coelenterates**
500 MILLION YEARS AGO

**Amphibians**
370 MILLION YEARS AGO

650 MILLION YEARS AGO (MYA) | 600 MYA | 550 MYA | 500 MYA | 450 MYA | 400 MYA | 350 MYA

**Sponges**
640 MILLION YEARS AGO

**Mollusks**
545 MILLION YEARS AGO

**MORE THAN** 700 million years ago, Earth was a much quieter place and was filled with simple organisms that could barely move. But as the Earth became more complex, animals developed traits that would help them thrive in their new environments. Below is a timeline of when specific animal groups first appeared. Scientists know these dates because they've found fossils from millions and millions of years ago!

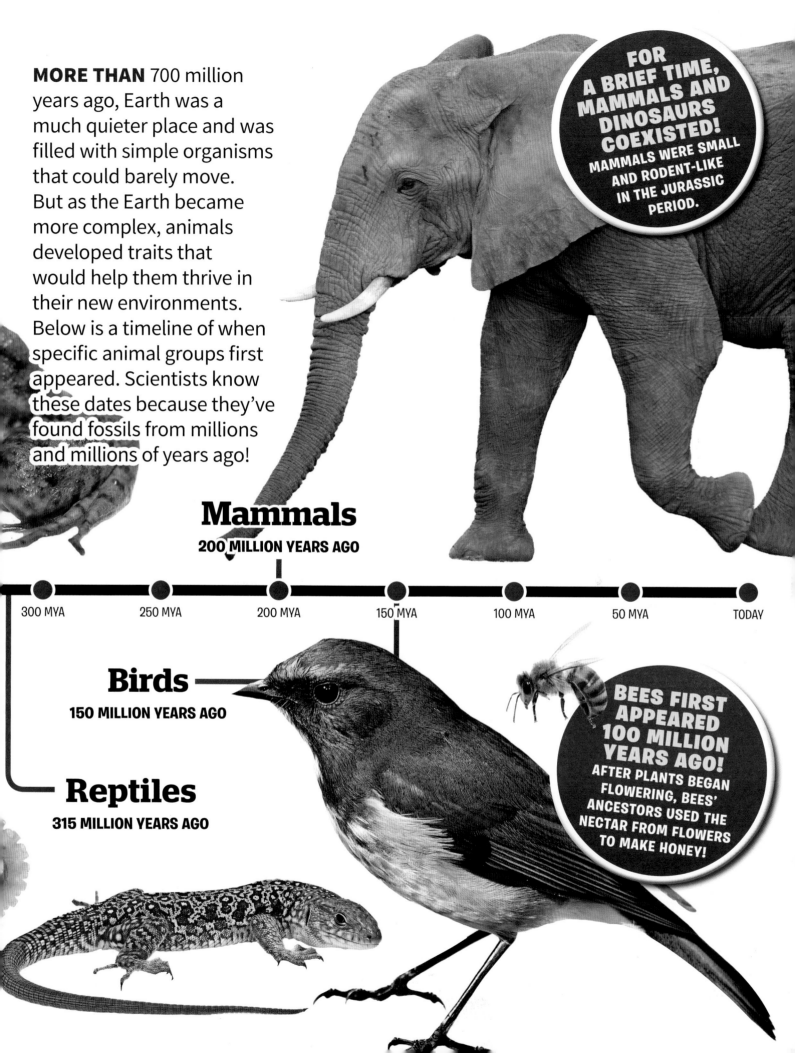

**FOR A BRIEF TIME, MAMMALS AND DINOSAURS COEXISTED!** MAMMALS WERE SMALL AND RODENT-LIKE IN THE JURASSIC PERIOD.

## Mammals
**200 MILLION YEARS AGO**

| 300 MYA | 250 MYA | 200 MYA | 150 MYA | 100 MYA | 50 MYA | TODAY |

## Birds
**150 MILLION YEARS AGO**

## Reptiles
**315 MILLION YEARS AGO**

**BEES FIRST APPEARED 100 MILLION YEARS AGO!** AFTER PLANTS BEGAN FLOWERING, BEES' ANCESTORS USED THE NECTAR FROM FLOWERS TO MAKE HONEY!

# A is for **Arctic**

**ANIMALS** that live in the Arctic need more than a fur coat and a pair of wool mittens to survive in sub-zero temperatures. Here's how they keep themselves from turning into animal-cicles in the northernmost region on Earth!

## Stoat

**THE STOAT** changes its coloring, which also functions as camouflage, with the seasons. Using its slim and short body to its advantage, the stoat easily bounds through the snow after its favorite meal, rabbits.

STOATS ARE FOUND IN COLDER CLIMATES WITH THE EXCEPTION OF NEW ZEALAND! THEY WERE INTRODUCED TO THE MORE TROPICAL CLIMATE TO CONTROL THE RABBIT POPULATION.

## Musk-Ox →

**TRUDGING ACROSS** the frozen tundra with their woolly coat and snacking on moss, the musk-ox stays near the Arctic Circle year-round. Although these 800-pound, furry cousins of cows might seem easygoing, they can hold their own against a pack of wolves.

## Walrus

**WHEN THEY GET HUNGRY,** walruses head to the seafloor in search of food. The sensitive whiskers on a walrus's face help it feel for food along the muddy floor. Worms, starfish and clams are among the animals consumed by these water mammals.

# A

is for **Arctic**

## Ribbon Seal

**DIVING AS DEEP** as 600 meters into the water, ribbon seals have a special air sac in their throats, which scientists think might help the seals float. They're most well-known for the white rings in their otherwise black and brown fur.

# Caribou

**WITH THEIR IMPRESSIVE** antlers and fur coat, caribou are right at home in Canada, Greenland and Northern Europe, but they still migrate south when the harsh Arctic winter begins. The undersides of the caribou's hooves are hollowed out so they can scoop snow out of the way to find food.

ALTHOUGH BABY HARP SEALS ARE KNOWN FOR THEIR FLUFFY WHITE FUR, THEY LOSE THAT FUR ABOUT 12 DAYS AFTER BEING BORN.

# Harp Seal

**WITH ITS EXCELLENT** swimming skills, the harp seal navigates frigid waters for shrimp and other fish. They can stay submerged for up to 15 minutes and spend most of their lives in the water, only coming to land to mate and raise their pups.

# A

is for **Arctic**

**ORCA TEETH CAN BE 4 INCHES LONG!**

## Arctic Foxes

**ALTHOUGH THESE RESILIENT CREATURES** are the size of an average dog, Arctic foxes are built for the cold weather. They can survive in temperatures as cold as -58 degrees F because they burrow under the ice to create a warm(er) hideaway and have fluffy white coats. But when the season changes to summer, Arctic foxes will adjust to the new season with a lighter, brown coat that blends into their new surroundings.

# Orca

**UNLIKE MANY OTHER** oceanic mammals, orcas hunt and take down other animals, such as walruses and blue whales, in large packs. One of the most aggressive species in the dolphin family, the orca is sometimes known as the "Killer Whale."

**ALTHOUGH THE MALE NARWHAL'S TUSK MIGHT LOOK LIKE A HORN,** IT'S ACTUALLY A 9-FOOT-LONG TOOTH THAT HAS 10 MILLION NERVE-ENDINGS!

# Narwhal

**A MEMBER OF THE PORPOISE SPECIES,** the narwhal primarily lives around the Arctic Circle. The narwhal has blubber, like other whales and seals, which helps it hold in its heat. They travel in groups of 15 to 20 and feed in open ice-free waters, where they snack on shrimp, squid and other fish.

# B is for Bipedal

**MANY ANIMALS NATURALLY** walk around on four legs, but some walk on two, just like people. These animals generally use their rear limbs to move around upright and use their upper arms or wings for balance. Hopping, walking and running are considered bipedal movements.

## ← Gibbon

**KNOWN AS THE** most bipedal of all the primates, the gibbon throws its arms above its head when walking on two feet in order to maintain balance. Although they are very comfortable on two feet, they can also swing through the trees at 35 mph.

## Quokka

**PART OF THE MACROPOD** family along with the kangaroo, the quokka is also anchored by its flat feet and long rat-like tail. Making its home in the swampy areas of Australia, the quokka emerges from its hideaway at night to hunt and explore.

# Ostrich

**REACHING UP TO 9 FEET TALL,** the ostrich holds the title of world's largest bird. While all birds are bipedal, the ostrich puts its legs to good use and can consistently maintain a speed of 31 mph. At just 1 month old, a baby ostrich can run almost as fast as its parents!

OSTRICHES LIVE IN AFRICA'S SAVANNAS AND DESERT LANDS! AT THE COLUMBUS ZOO, THIS OSTRICH CAN BE FOUND IN THE HEART OF AFRICA REGION!

Ostriches hold their wings out for balance. This allows them to change directions quickly!

# B

is for **Bipedal**

CHIMPANZEES CAN LEARN SIGN LANGUAGE TO COMMUNICATE WITH EACH OTHER AND HUMANS!

## Chimpanzee ⟶

**THE CHIMPANZEE** alternates between walking on two feet and four, but they do feel more comfortable walking around on their knuckles and feet than bipedally. Chimpanzees are one of the most intelligent primates, using tools to break open nuts.

A CHIMP ON ALL FOURS!

## Springhare

**APPEARING TO BE** a cross between a rabbit and a kangaroo, the springhare springs up to 6 feet forward on its two legs when it feels threatened. Found in Africa, they have sharp claws used to dig into the earth to make a burrow.

## Spider Monkey

**WHEN THE SPIDER MONKEY** isn't hanging around in trees, it walks around on the ground on two legs. But that doesn't mean the spider monkey prefers this means of transportation. It would much rather be using its prehensile tail, which can grip tree limbs and help the monkey swing from tree to tree.

# B is for Bipedal

## Kangaroo

**USING THEIR LARGE** flat feet as trampolines, kangaroos can propel themselves forward 30 feet in a single bound. But they're not only far jumpers, they're also fast jumpers, reaching speeds of 30 mph. Although kangaroos are bipedal, their tails act like a third limb and keep them from losing their balance.

**WHEN BABY KANGAROOS (AKA JOEYS) ARE BORN, THEY ARE THE SIZE OF A GRAPE!**

## Atlantic Puffin

**ADMIRED FOR ITS** bright orange beak, this bird primarily uses its webbed feet for diving into the depths of the Atlantic to eat herring or sand eels. But these birds aren't only built for the sea; by flapping their wings 400 times per minute, they can reach speeds of up to 55 mph.

# Peacock

**THE MALE MEMBERS** of the peafowl species are at their most magnificent when standing with their green, blue and brown tail feathers spread out. This train of feathers is 60 inches long, which is 10 inches longer than the peacock's body. If necessary, the peacock has the ability to detach the majority of its tail and fly away from predators.

# C is for **Camouflage**

**CAMOUFLAGE** is the use of any combination of materials, coloration or illumination that either hides an animal by helping it blend in with its surroundings or makes it look like something else entirely. Certain animals are able to alter their shape or color to mimic what's around them, making even predators with the keenest of eyes overlook them.

## Leafy Sea Dragon

**IN THE OCEAN** there aren't many places to hide, but sea dragons can live unnoticed in the open water. These sea creatures are born with numerous green-brown appendages, which look like leaves. They float at a slow pace or even let the current take them, appearing to be seaweed as they drift.

MIMICKING A SQUID!

## Mimic Octopus

**THIS SPECIES** of octopus is the king of camouflage. The mimic octopus can change color and scrunch itself to impersonate at least 10 different dangerous creatures and inanimate objects, including conch shells, squid or even sand!

# Screech Owl

**NOT ONLY DO** land and sea creatures use camouflage, birds do too! Because the screech owl sleeps during the day, it needs to be inconspicuous while it rests. The owl's brown, white and gray feathers help it blend seamlessly into the trees, where owls live and make their nests.

**BLENDING IN WITH SAND!**

**MASQUERADING AS A CONCH SHELL!**

**ANIMALS USUALLY USE CAMOUFLAGE FOR TWO REASONS:** THEY EITHER WANT TO BLEND INTO THEIR NATURAL HABITATS OR THEY PRETEND TO BE ANOTHER, MORE DANGEROUS ANIMAL.

# C is for Camouflage

## Scarlet Kingsnake

**THE SCARLET KINGSNAKE'S** striped bands of red, yellow and black can send both animals and people running. Although the kingsnake is not actually venomous, it uses camouflage to mimic its much more dangerous relative, the coral snake.

**A SHY SNAKE, THE SCARLET KINGSNAKE AVOIDS EVERYONE.** ALTHOUGH THEY'RE GREAT MIMICS, THEY ARE RARELY SEEN. KINGSNAKES PREFER TO HIDE UNDER ROCKS OR BENEATH TREE BARK.

THE DEADLY CORAL SNAKE!

There are several rhymes you can memorize to help determine whether you're encountering a coral snake or scarlet kingsnake in North America. Here's my personal favorite: "If red touches yellow, you're a dead fellow; if red touches black, you're all right, Jack."

## Walking Stick

**IN ORDER TO** stay safe from bug-hungry predators, the walking stick blends in with its surroundings. As its name suggests, this insect looks just like a stick. The walking stick even sways back and forth like a twig would in the wind!

## Hawk Moth

**MOTHS AND BUTTERFLIES** are usually very vulnerable when they're feeding on flowers, but not the hawk moth. With its intricate wing patterns, the hawk moth appears to be part of the stem, leaves or flower of the plant to which it's attached.

# C is for Camouflage

## Leopard

**PERCHED HIGH** up in a tree, the leopard is able to survey its prey without being seen. Their spotted coats help them hide among the leaves. By the time the leopard pounces down from the tree and reveals itself, it's far too late for the prey to get away.

THORN BUGS WILL OFTEN CLUSTER TOGETHER ON PLANT STEMS, OR EVEN TREE TRUNKS, AND SUCK THE SAP OUT OF THE PLANT. NOT ONLY DO THEY LOOK LIKE THORNS, THEY CAN ALSO DAMAGE AND KILL PLANTS BE PIERCING THE PLANT TISSUE.

## Thorn Bug

**MUCH LIKE** the thorn bug's name suggests, it appears as if a thorn is sticking right out of this bug's head. Although the "thorn" is not actually sharp or dangerous to other bugs and animals, a larger bug or bird won't risk getting poked or stuck by it.

# Viceroy Butterfly

**IF YOU CAN'T** beat 'em, join 'em. At least, that's the Viceroy butterfly's attitude toward staying alive. With its red, black and white wings, the Viceroy looks almost identical to its poisonous cousin, the Monarch butterfly (check it out in the M for Migration section!). Hunters look at the Viceroy butterfly and decide that they don't want to try their luck.

# D is for Domesticated

**ANIMALS HAVE ALWAYS** played a role in our lives. Many years ago, when certain animals realized people would give them nourishment, we were able to bring them into our lives to live with us side by side.

## Ferret

**DESCENDED FROM POLECATS,** ferrets became pets about 2,500 years ago. Approximately the same size and shape as a zucchini, this critter sleeps for 18 hours a day and was originally tasked with keeping rats out of barns and off ships. Although other domesticated animals are capable of surviving in the wild, ferrets can only last a few days without human care.

## Goat

**THE ONLY THING** a domesticated goat needs is some grass to munch on and a place to sleep; because of this, domesticated goats are all over the world. They were first domesticated 9,000 years ago for their ability to make milk and cheese. Their wild cousins in North America, mountain goats, live apart from humans in the Rocky Mountains.

# Dog

**MAN'S BEST FRIEND** has been around for thousands of years. Descendants of wolves, dogs are strong and loyal, making them perfect companions. A long time ago, people domesticated dogs because they helped us hunt and killed unwanted vermin. In more recent years, humans have selectively bred dogs to make them even more adorable.

RESPONSIBLE PET OWNERSHIP IS SO IMPORTANT. OUR DOGS HAVE ALWAYS BEEN PART OF THE FAMILY!

Dogs were the first animal humans ever domesticated! About 30,000 years ago, some species of wolves were warming up to humans. Scientists believe wolves started to rummage through our leftovers and began relying on us for food instead of hunting on their own.

# D

is for **Domesticated**

## Donkey →

**THE DONKEY** became one of our ways of getting around 6,000 years ago! Great at lifting heavy loads and traveling long distances, donkeys are still used today all over the world. In America, they're primarily pets and sometimes guard sheep.

I BROUGHT A DONKEY TO COLLEGE WITH ME— AND SUZI MARCHED WITH HIM IN THE HOMECOMING PARADE!

DONKEYS PREFER WARM, DRY CLIMATES.

# Pigeon

**ALTHOUGH MANY PEOPLE** see the pigeon as a pest in large U.S. cities, the domesticated pigeon has been extremely important during times of war. Five thousand years ago in Ancient Egypt, pigeons were used to deliver messages. They continued to do so until just after World War II because of their awesome navigational skills. Pigeons are sensitive to the Earth's magnetic field!

A PIGEON NAMED G.I. JOE WAS GIVEN THE DICKIN MEDAL. DURING WORLD WAR II IN ITALY, G.I. JOE FLEW 20 MILES IN 20 MINUTES TO DELIVER A MESSAGE THAT PLANES WERE ABOUT TO DROP BOMBS. THIS HEROIC PIGEON SAVED THE ENTIRE TOWN!

# Water Buffalo

**PRIMARILY FOUND** in the tropical jungles of India, the water buffalo has been domesticated for 5,000 years. Like cows in America, water buffalo produce dairy products and are eaten, but they also are relied upon to transport goods and plow fields. There are still wild water buffalo, but their numbers are dwindling.

# D

## is for **Domesticated**

## Yak

**FOUND PRIMARILY** in Tibet, the yak is an expert at scaling mountains in Mongolia, Tibet and Nepal. While most people would get dizzy in the high altitudes, the yak is just fine with its large set of lungs. Similar to America's horses, yak racing and yak polo are popular sports in Asia and the Middle East!

## Chicken

**THE CHICKEN** as we know it today has been around for roughly 7,000 years and was the first bird to be domesticated. At first, they appeared as exotic birds in Egypt and their eggs were considered delicacies. Today, there are billions of chickens in farms around the world! There are still wild species of chicken in Africa and Asia.

ALPACAS LOVE TO EAT FRESH GRASS!

ALPACAS DESIGNATE BATHROOM SPACE FOR THE ENTIRE HERD, SO IT DOESN'T INTERFERE WITH THEIR CLEAN, GRAZING GRASS.

# Alpaca →

**COUSINS OF THE LLAMA,** alpacas were domesticated thousands of years ago. They were first found in South America, but they've been sent to live in countries all over the world. All they need is a little bit of farmland to be happy! Today, these animals are kept for their soft wool, which people use to make clothing. There are no alpacas in the wild today.

WHEN I VISIT MONTANA DURING THE SUMMER, YOU CAN USUALLY FIND ME SPENDING TIME WITH MY ANIMALS—ALPACAS INCLUDED!

**ORANGUTANS ARE HIGHLY INTELLIGENT AND HAVE 97 PERCENT OF THE SAME GENES WE HAVE.**

BY MIMICKING HUMANS, ORANGUTANS HAVE LEARNED TO SAW WOOD, USE SOAP AND USE SIGN LANGUAGE!

# Orangutan

**RENOWNED FOR ITS** reddish-orange hair, the orangutan's name translates to "person of the forest" in English. Extraordinarily smart and handy with tools, an orangutan's arms can be as much as 2 feet longer than its entire body! These solitary creatures are endangered because their homes, which are primarily tropical forests, are being destroyed by deforestation.

# E is for **Endangered**

**FOR VARIOUS REASONS,** many species are struggling to survive. Fortunately, there are many people around the world working to keep these animals from becoming extinct.

## Sumatran Rhino

**WHILE THEY** are massive mammals, the Sumatran rhino is actually the smallest of all rhinoceroses in the world today. Sadly, their population is among the smallest as well, with only 220–275 currently in the wild. The dense highlands and tropical forests of Singapore are where the majority of these rare rhinos live.

## ← Dugong

**THIS SPECIES** of manatee, which lives off the coast of Asia, Australia and eastern Africa, is believed to be the inspiration for the mermaid myth thanks to its whale-like tail. Because dugongs aren't the swiftest of swimmers and spend most of their time grazing, they are an easy target for hunters.

**ALTHOUGH ONE LIVES UNDER THE SEA AND THE OTHER LIVES IN THE SAHARA, THE DUGONG AND THE ELEPHANT ARE ACTUALLY RELATED!**

# E is for Endangered

The axolotl has a rare characteristic called neoteny that makes it resemble its tadpole form as an adult. Unlike other salamanders, the axolotl has its gills on the outside of its body and a fin running down its back!

## Axolotl

**THERE'S ONLY ONE** place in the world where you can find these salamanders: Lake Xochimilco. The axolotl, which can reach up to a foot long, lives in this lake near Mexico City. Because it has the rare ability to regrow lost limbs, scientists are scrambling to find out this water salamander's secrets! But axolotls are rapidly heading toward extinction due to a contaminated habitat and overhunting—they're considered a delicacy in Mexico.

# Sea Turtle

**THE SEA TURTLE** has been swimming in our oceans for 110 million years—since dinosaurs roamed the Earth! With an ability to spend more than five hours underwater, the sea turtle has one of the longest migrations and can travel more than 1,400 miles to lay eggs. Sea turtles lay eggs on the beach, which makes their young susceptible to predators.

THIS AFRICAN PAINTED DOG LIVES AT THE WILDS , A 10,000-ACRE CONSERVATION CENTER IN OHIO AND A PARTNER OF THE COLUMBUS ZOO!

AFRICAN PAINTED DOGS PROTECT THEIR OWN!
IF THERE'S AN ILL OR OLDER MEMBER OF THEIR PACK, THEY WILL HUNT AND GATHER FOOD FOR THEM.

# African Painted Dog

**A PACK ANIMAL** that roams the Sahara, the African painted dog's habitat is shrinking as humans begin to tame wild land and build homes. African painted dogs hunt in packs, ranging in number from 6–20 dogs, and take down larger prey, such as wildebeests.

# E is for Endangered

## Saola

**DESPITE BEING DISCOVERED** only 25 years ago, the saola is already critically endangered. During an expedition in the Annamite Mountains in Vietnam and Laos, explorers stumbled upon the saola, which looks like an antelope with its impressive set of 20-inch horns. Scientists were shocked to learn there were still undiscovered mammals!

## Pangolin

**ALTHOUGH IT LOOKS** like a cross between an armadillo and anteater, the pangolin is unique: It's the only mammal in the world covered in scales! These scales are made out of the same material as rhino horns and even our fingernails: keratin. When threatened, the pangolin will protect its face and underside by rolling itself up into a ball. This species is one of the most illegally trafficked animals in the world and is critically endangered.

Because pangolins don't have any teeth, they rely on their tongues to collect insects. At up to 16 inches, the pangolin's tongue can be longer than its entire body! It devours roughly 70 million insects a year.

# Mongoose

**WITH A LONG BODY** and short snout, the mongoose spends most of its time in burrows. These mammals prefer to live in groups and aren't picky predators. They've been famously known to tango with and take down cobras. Mongeese are endangered because they are losing their natural habitat.

**MONGEESE ARE MOSTLY FOUND IN AFRICA!**

**MONGEESE ARE SMARTER THAN THEY LOOK!** THEY WILL THROW BIRD EGGS AGAINST A SOLID OBJECT, CRACKING THE EGGS OPEN TO EAT WHAT'S INSIDE.

# F is for Flight

**THE ABILITY TO FLY** is always an advantage for animals, and it's used by more than just birds! Whether they use their skills to hunt prey or to travel at high speeds or long distances, flight is an incredibly important trait in the daily lives of many species.

## Spine-Tailed Swift

**WHEN IT FLIES** at a steady level, the spine-tailed swift is the fastest bird on the planet. On average, it can travel at speeds up to 105 miles per hour! That amazing flight speed allows the spine-tailed swift to catch thousands of airborne insects a day.

# Hummingbird

**THEY MAY BE TINY,** but hummingbirds possess some impressive flying skills. In normal flight, the North American hummingbird beats its wings about 53 times per second. They're also the only birds capable of flying backward!

WE FILMED THIS HUMMINGBIRD IN ITS NATIVE HABITAT IN ECUADOR WHILE FILMING FOR JACK HANNA'S INTO THE WILD IN 2015!

Sugar gliders can sustain flight long enough to glide the length of an entire football field!

# Sugar Glider

**ALTHOUGH THIS LITTLE** creature weighs less than one pound, it loves feeding on nectar and tree sap and will go a long way to satisfy its sweet tooth—probably even farther than you! Like a flying squirrel, the sugar glider has skin flaps that act as wings so it can fly, or rather, fall with style.

 **is for
Flight**

## Bald Eagle

**THE NATIONAL BIRD OF** the United States of America can be found near any major body of water! Bald eagles are capable of diving at up to 100 mph to grab a fish with its talons, but they will also snatch up and eat small mammals.

**BALD EAGLE MATES PAIR OFF FOR LIFE.** UNLIKE MOST OTHER ANIMALS, EAGLES SEEK OUT THEIR SOULMATES. AFTER FINDING A PARTNER, THEY BUILD THEIR NEST TOGETHER.

## Northern Flying Squirrel

**THESE "FLYING" SQUIRRELS** technically glide but can still cover distances of more than 150 feet. Northern flying squirrels have a special skin that puts wind beneath their flaps, enabling them to stay aloft.

# Flying Frog

**THE FLYING FROG** might sound like something that would only exist in a science fiction movie, but they are actually real. They spend most of their lives up in trees, and have developed a technique over time to get from branch to branch. By unfurling the skin between their feet, they're able to fly for up to 50 feet!

After these frogs are done gliding, sticking the landing is easy! Flying frogs have sticky feet that keep them from falling off any trees.

is for
**Flight**

# Rüppell's Vulture

**HOLDING THE RECORD** for highest flier, Rüppell's vultures can reach 37,000 feet! Next time you're flying on an airplane, don't be alarmed if you see a vulture out your window. Humans would pass out from lack of oxygen at those heights, but Rüppell's vultures are able to use oxygen much more effectively than other animals.

# Erigone Spider

**FOR PEOPLE WHO** are afraid of spiders, they might not want to read this entry. There are flying spiders, but they don't quite have wings. On top of using their webs to trap prey, erigone spiders are able to knit small silk webs to use as little air balloons, allowing them to travel many miles.

# Dragonfly

**WITH THE ABILITY** to hover in the air like a helicopter and fly up and down, the dragonfly is an expert flier. Their four wings give them maximum control, allowing them to zip and hover. Interestingly, they can only eat if they're flying.

Dragonflies were one of the first insects. They've been around for 300 million years!

# G

## is for
## Group Living

**WHILE NATURE CERTAINLY** has its solitary roamers, some animals prefer to live with a whole bunch of members of their species. They eat together, play together, find food together and even look after each other, like a family! At the Columbus Zoo and Aquarium, there are three family groups of lowland gorillas. The matriarch of one of these families is the oldest gorilla in human care—her name is Colo and she was born at the Columbus Zoo in 1956!

**USUALLY A TROOP OF GORILLAS RANGES FROM 5 TO 10 GORILLAS, BUT THEIR FAMILIES CAN BE AS LARGE AS 50!**

## Velvet Worms

**ALTHOUGH THEY MIGHT** not look very velvety, their colorful skin is completely water-repellant! These worms have been around for 500 million years and haven't changed their behavior much in that time. Ruled by one dominant female who always feeds first, velvet worms live in groups of up to 15.

## Vampire Bat

**UNLIKE THE MYTHICAL** monster these creatures are associated with, vampire bats don't live alone in creepy castles—but they do feed off of blood! They live in large groups, ranging from 100 to 1,000 bats. A group of 100 bats can consume all of the blood from 25 cows in just one year.

## Gorilla

**SOME ANIMALS SIMPLY** enjoy each other's company, but the gorilla has its own government or social structure. The largest male will lead the troop for many years alongside the most dominant female gorilla. They're almost like a king and queen!

# G is for Group Living

## Rhesus Macaque

**FOUND IN MOST ASIAN COUNTRIES,** the rhesus macaque lives in huge colonies of 200 monkeys. Unlike many group animals, the rhesus macaque has female leaders. This small monkey is so smart that it's even learned how to interact with humans to bargain for food!

**THEY'RE HUNGRY, HUNGRY ELEPHANTS!** ELEPHANTS EAT BETWEEN 300 AND 400 POUNDS OF FOOD A DAY! THEY'RE NOT TOO PICKY EITHER. ELEPHANTS EAT GRASS, ROOTS AND BANANAS!

## Hyena

**STANDING JUST OVER** 2.5 feet tall, a single hyena doesn't seem like much of a threat to the much-larger zebra. But a pack of hyenas can take down and eat a zebra in less than half an hour.

## Elephant

**WHILE THE SIZE** of an elephant herd varies, the fact that it's mostly comprised of female elephants and children does not. A matriarch leads the group of female elephants. Male elephants are usually solitary and only travel with the herd for a brief amount of time.

# G is for
## Group Living

## Sun Conure

**THE SUN CONURE LIVES IN GROUPS** of 10 to 30 birds! When they all fly together, they resemble the setting sun. But these bright birds aren't born with their sunset-hued feathers. The sun conure has green feathers when it's a baby, letting it blend into foliage and stay out of sight.

## Meerkat

**BEING A MEERKAT** is a lot of work. Because they're essentially defenseless against predators, meerkats choose to live in large groups comprised of several families. While living in a complex system of burrows, meerkats have specific tasks. Some hunt and others keep a lookout for predators, warning their group in case danger arrives.

# Dolphin

**DOLPHINS ARE VERY** social and intelligent marine mammals that live in groups called schools or pods. Not only are they friendly to people, they will also help care for an injured dolphin outside of their pod.

DOLPHINS NAME THEMSELVES WITH A SPECIAL CLICK OR SQUEAL! THEY REFER TO THEMSELVES BY IT AND ALSO CALL OTHER DOLPHINS BY THEIR "NAMES."

# H

## is for **Hooves**

**HOOVED ANIMALS** have hard or rubber-like-soled feet, with each toe encapsulated by a giant nail. Hooves have their advantages, either helping an animal maneuver in its terrain, move quickly or support its weight.

## Zebra

**AS ONE OF THE LION'S** favorite meals, the zebra has to take off at a moment's notice. When a zebra herd runs together, their black and white stripes help keep predators confused about how many zebras there actually are. However, away from the herd, this zebra at the Columbus Zoo and Aquarium sure stands out!

# Gazelle

**A MEMBER OF** the antelope family, gazelles gather in large groups in the African plains to graze for food. In order to escape predators, gazelles zig, zag and sprint away at their top speed of 40 mph.

# Horse

**WITH MORE THAN** 400 breeds spanning every continent except Antarctica, horses are literally all over the world. Both domesticated and wild, horses have been around for millions of years. These hooved animals can reach speeds of 30 mph and can cover 25–30 miles a day, even if they're pulling a wagon.

Domesticated horses are fitted with metal horseshoes so their feet are protected from wear and tear!

# H is for Hooves

## Tapir

**THE TAPIR,** which lives in South America, spends many hours cooling off in the water. Their hooves keep them from getting stuck in the mud and are filled with fat to help absorb shock when they run!

TAPIRS LIKE TAKING THE PATH WELL-TRAVELED, USUALLY CREATED BY THEM OR OTHER MEMBERS OF THEIR SPECIES!

In 2010, I filmed tapirs for *Jack Hanna's Into the Wild* at the Taricaya Rescue Center in Peru with Suzi and two of my daughters, Suzanne and Julie!

# Llama

**THESE WOOLY CREATURES** live primarily in the wild in Peru. Llamas are domesticated all over the world and are sometimes used as pack animals—their hooves are excellent for helping them traverse the mountainous terrain. But when a llama is overloaded, it will lie down and refuse to move. If you're unlucky, it will also hiss or spit.

# Giraffe

**ALTHOUGH GIRAFFES** might look as though they would trip over their own long limbs, they can run 35 mph! They've got large hooves, helping their feet support up to 2,800 pounds of body weight.

**H** is for **Hooves**

## Bison

**WEIGHING MORE THAN** one ton, a bison uses its feet to put up with quite a lot of weight. But don't let their size fool you—they can run at speeds of 40 mph, thanks in part to their hooves. Bison spend most of their time grazing on the plains of North America.

## Markhor

**A RELATIVE OF** the goat family, this unusual hooved animal lives up in central Asian mountains. They use their hooves to grip the rocky landscape they so often scale and have no problem surviving 3,500 meters above ground. I've seen markhors in action at the Columbus Zoo and Aquarium, and they sure can climb!

**DURING PERIODS OF DROUGHT,** A GEMSBOK WILL USE ITS HOOVES TO DIG UP TUBERS AND ROOTS, WHICH PROVIDE IT WITH HYDRATION.

# Gemsbok

**WITH AN IMPRESSIVE** set of horns that are up to five feet long, the gemsbok becomes a fierce adversary when it encounters a predator. Unlike many species of horned animals, both female and male gemsbok have horns.

Bison digest their food twice! They chew, swallow and regurgitate plants before eating them for a second time.

# I is for **Insects**

**THEY MAY NOT** take up much space individually, but insects are capable of incredible feats and there are an estimated 10 quintillion of them on the planet!

## Lightning Bug

**USUALLY SEEN** in the summertime, lightning bugs (also known as fireflies) can be identified by the glowing golden light their bodies create. These insects produce a pattern of flashes in order to attract mates. Scientists think their light may also function as a defense mechanism, broadcasting to predators that they're not very tasty!

LIGHTNING BUGS ARE A TYPE OF BEETLE!

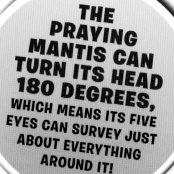

# Praying Mantis

**ONE OF THE MOST** effective hunters in the insect kingdom, the praying mantis has an arsenal of physical attributes to capture its breakfast, lunch and dinner. The mantis blends in with its grassy homeland and silently stalks its unassuming prey on four thin back legs while its prominent arms grab its meal— faster than the human eye can see! When the praying mantis's arms are occupied, its back legs can act as spears to stab through prey.

# Desert Locust

**A RELATIVE OF** the grasshopper, the desert locust is a particularly pesky insect. When they unite as a group, desert locusts can form swarms stretching up to 460 square miles! A swarm that size can eat about 423 million pounds of plants in just one day, making the desert locust a major agricultural threat.

# I is for Insects

## Flea

**ALTHOUGH THIS INSECT** is incredibly tiny, it can be very irritating! Only growing up to .39 inches long, fleas are parasites that feed off the blood of birds, rodents, pets and sometimes even humans! Their bites cause itchiness, and once they've made their home in the coat of another animal, they refuse to be evicted without heavy doses of medication.

**A TERMITE QUEEN CAN LAY 30,000 EGGS A DAY!**

## Termite

**FIRST APPEARING** 130 million years ago, this insect has been on Earth for a long time! Infamous for eating through the wood in people's homes, termites live in large colonies, usually in wooded areas. Similar to ants, termites have a queen and thousands of worker termites that wait on her.

> Most insects are not protective of their young, but stink bugs are! Mothers will fight predators away from their eggs.

## Stink Bug

**DESPITE BEING NAMED** the stink bug, its odor is not this insect's most pesky trait. Stink bugs love eating fruits, vegetables and other plants. During harvest season, farmers often find these stinkers have taken bites out of their crop. When these insects are squashed and killed, they emit a gross odor, earning their name!

**DUNG BEETLES CAN LIFT 1,141 TIMES THEIR OWN WEIGHT!**

# Dung Beetle

**RATHER THAN SCOURING** the earth for fresh, undigested food, the dung beetle prefers to eat animal waste, making it one of the weirder creatures of the animal kingdom. The dung beetle will roll animal poop into balls, either saving it for later nourishment or using it as a place to lay eggs!

# Long-Nosed Weevil

**WITH A SURPRISINGLY** stretched-out snout, the long-nosed weevil gives Pinocchio a run for his money! At the end of the weevil's snout is a sharp pair of mandibles that it uses to chew plants. Like many other plant-eating insects, weevils cause problems for crops and stored foods.

# Assassin Bug

**THIS SPIKY INSECT** is an expert predator, hunting down ants and termites for its meals. But the assassin bug doesn't just paralyze and eat its prey; it has a special, sticky exoskeleton and prefers to carry the corpses of its meal on its back.

THE ASSASSIN BUG USES ITS PILE OF COLLECTED BUGS AS CAMOUFLAGE. A HUNGRY PREDATOR IS MORE LIKELY TO GET A MOUTHFUL OF DEAD ANTS THAN THE ASSASSIN BUG IT WAS CRAVING.

# Musk Deer →

**FAMOUS FOR ITS** two protruding fangs, the male musk deer looks like it decided to dress up as a vampire for Halloween. Actually, if you see a musk deer with fangs, that means it's mating season. Musk deer use their fangs to fight off other males competing for the same partner.

# Tiger

**ONE OF THE MOST** majestic predators in the jungle, the tiger uses its speed, claws and razor-sharp teeth to bring down prey. Sometimes, tigers just use their teeth to grab a hold of their prey, but their set of 30 pearly whites can also chew through bone. Tigers are born without teeth, but they develop a set just a few days later.

# J is for **Jaws**

**A JAW IS OFTEN** the first tool in the digestive process, chewing up food so it can be swallowed more easily. Although most animals only use this complicated set of bones to break down food like we do, some use their powerful jaws to help bring down prey, scare off predators or secure a mate!

## Great White Shark

**WITH MORE THAN** 300 serrated teeth, the great white shark can tear through just about anything that crosses its path. If they lose a tooth now and then, it's no big deal: They just keep regrowing them!

THE ONE THING THESE SHARKS DON'T DO IS CHEW. THEY USE THEIR TEETH TO RIP, BUT THEN THEY SWALLOW THEIR MEALS WHOLE!

# J

is for **Jaws**

## Alligator

**THIS REPTILIAN SWAMP DWELLER** has a long, thin jaw, housing anywhere from 70 to 84 teeth at one time. With a vicious snap, an alligator can break the shell of a snapping turtle in half.

**IF YOU'VE EVER WONDERED HOW TO TELL AN ALLIGATOR AND CROCODILE APART, JUST LOOK AT THE TEETH!**
AN ALLIGATOR'S TEETH ARE NOT VISIBLE WHEN ITS MOUTH IS CLOSED, WHILE YOU CAN SEE SEVERAL TEETH PROTRUDING FROM A CROC'S CLOSED MOUTH.

## Babirusa

**PLAYFULLY NICKNAMED THE** "deer-pig," the babirusa has two sets of tusks protruding from its head! Rather than just fighting other members of its own species or fending off larger predators, the babirusa uses its tusks to plow through the sand and dirt. In addition to the tusks, the babirusa's jaws are strong enough to help them crack through nuts!

# Burmese Python

**UNLIKE MOST OTHER SNAKES,** the Burmese python does not strike a fatal blow to its prey with its teeth. Instead, this python uses its fangs to grip the animal and then coils its body around the prey to strangle it. Once its prey is ready to eat, the python will swallow its food whole. Thanks to stretchy ligaments in their jaws, Burmese pythons can swallow animals five times as wide as their head!

CHECK OUT THE CROCODILE TEETH!

# J

is for **Jaws**

## Alligator Snapping Turtle

**ON TOP OF** having a jaw encased in a sharp beak made for ripping flesh, the alligator snapping turtle's mouth boasts a neat trick. Its tongue has a red, worm-shaped piece of flesh which it uses to lure fish right into its mouth!

## Mastiff

**WITH THE LARGEST** head and widest mouth out of any dog breed, it isn't surprising that the mastiff has one of the strongest sets of jaws as well. Although this dog is a loyal and normally gentle pet, it can definitely defend itself. The mastiff's bite exerts 552 pounds of power, which is almost as powerful as a lion's bite!

Alligator snapping turtles are not picky eaters! They'll eat anything from small aquatic animals like frogs and crayfish to larger animals, like raccoons and armadillos.

**CHECK OUT ITS BUILT-IN LURE!**

# Common Merganser

**A BIRD'S JAW** is its beak! One of the few birds that has anything resembling teeth, the common merganser has an advantage over other ducks when it comes to securing dinner. Their bills have serrated edges that they use to keep a grip on slippery fish and crack open the mollusks and crustaceans they feed on.

# K

## is for **Kooky**

**THESE ANIMALS** might be notable for looking weird, but that's not the only spectacular thing about them.

### Giant Isopod

**ALTHOUGH THIS MIGHT** look like the largest bug you've ever seen, isopods are actually related to crabs and shellfish! It's called a giant isopod because they can get as long as 2.5 feet. They live deep at the bottom of the ocean where they spend most of their time buried in the sand.

**GIANT ISOPODS CAN GO AT LEAST ONE YEAR WITHOUT EATING ANYTHING!**

## Olm  Salamander

**EXTRAORDINARILY RARE,** this blind water-dwelling salamander lives in the caves of the Balkans. Researchers believe these strange salamanders live for 100 years and only reproduce once every 10 to 20 years!

# Seahorse

**UNLIKE MOST ANIMALS** on the planet, the male seahorse carries and gives birth to its young. The female seahorse still produces the eggs, but she gives them to the male, who has a special pouch in which he carries them until they hatch!

**SEAHORSES LIVE IN SHALLOW TROPICAL WATERS!**

Because they're so bony and hard to digest, the seahorse has very few natural predators.

# K is for Kooky

## Red-Lipped Batfish

**FOUND LIVING UNDER THE SEA** near the Galápagos Islands, the red-lipped batfish looks like someone smeared lipstick all over its mouth, and no one knows why! This fish also has a habit of "walking" around on the ocean floor with its pectoral fins.

## Naked Mole Rat

**WITH PROMINENT TEETH** that make it look a bit like a tiny walrus, the naked mole rat is far from the cutest of rodents . Nearly blind, the naked mole rat stays beneath the East African dirt with its colony. One of the only mammal species to have a "queen" like insects do, some worker rats spend their time digging tunnels and gathering food, while others tend to their queen.

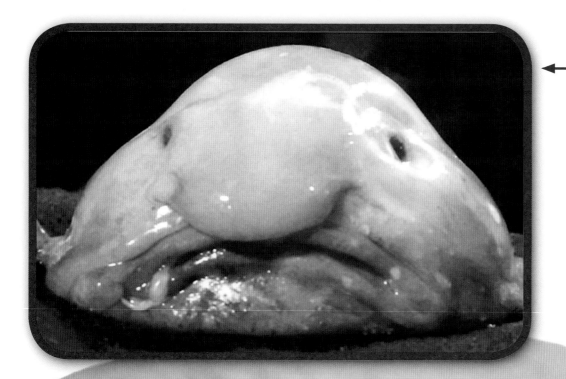

## Blobfish

**THE APTLY NAMED** blobfish lives deep in the waters off the coast of Australia. Because it lives far down in the ocean where the pressure is extremely high, it wouldn't survive with a skeleton or muscles!

Even though its name has "naked" in the title, these rodents are not actually hairless! They have about 100 fine hairs that act as whiskers and help them feel around the tunnels they create.

# K

is for
**Kooky**

## Lamprey →

**THIS UNDERSEA CREATURE** is an extremely primitive vertebrate, with a skeleton made of cartilage rather than bone. It looks a lot like an eel, until you notice that it doesn't have a jaw! Instead, these sea creatures have round, sucker-like mouths.

## Bush Viper

**NATIVE TO CENTRAL AFRICA,** the bush viper does an excellent job of blending into its habitat, thanks to scales that look exactly like tiny leaves. This venomous reptile is an agile climber and feeds on small mammals, frogs and lizards.

## Yeti Crab

**IF A FISH OR CRAB** is going to live more than 2,000 meters below the ocean in the Antarctic, it might as well have a coat like the yeti crab. Technically not hair, these stiff bristles trap bacteria, which the yeti crab eats!

The bush viper is extremely polymorphic, meaning it occurs in many different colors! Bush vipers can be red, orange, blue, gray, yellow, black, brown or green.

# L is for **Lazy**

**NATURE HAS ITS** fair share of animals that love nothing more than lying around. Some spend more of their days asleep than awake!

ARMADILLOS ARE THE ONLY MAMMALS THAT HAVE A SHELL! ALTHOUGH IT MIGHT LOOK LIKE ALL ARMADILLOS CAN CURL UP INTO A BALL, ONLY ONE TYPE CAN. THE REST JUST USE THEIR SHELL TO STAY SAFE.

## Armadillo

**THIS SHELLED ANIMAL** burrows deep in the desert dirt to take 16-hour naps. The armadillo has a low metabolic rate and can get tired easily, so they save their energy for finding food during the early morning—and then it's back to bed!

# Koala

**KOALAS ARE CUTE,** cuddly and absolutely lazy. They spend 18 to 22 hours asleep in the eucalyptus trees they love so much! When they do finally wake, they spend the majority of their time eating.

# Cat

**ONE OF THE MOST** common household pets in the United States, the cat can usually be found curled up, snoozing away. But they aren't as lazy as you might think. Cats are very active at night! Some studies actually suggest that cats allowed themselves to be domesticated because it was easier than staying wild.

# L is for Lazy

## Hamster

**COMPLETELY DOMESTIC** and undeniably cuddly, hamsters rely on humans to fulfill all of their needs. Although they might use their plastic tunnels or run in their wheels from time to time, they spend 18 hours of their day napping.

THE ECHIDNA IS A MAMMAL, BUT IT LAYS EGGS LIKE A BIRD! THE FEMALE ECHIDNA WILL LAY THE EGG IN ITS POUCH, WHERE IT INCUBATES FOR 10 DAYS.

## Echidna

**WITH A SET OF SPINES** that would deter most predators from trying to take a bite, the echidna doesn't need to expend energy to run away. It can just burrow down and take a 12-hour nap to wait the predator out!

**LEMURS ARE THE ONLY PRIMATES THAT SLEEP IN CAVES EVERY NIGHT!**

# Ring-Tailed Lemur

**LIVING SOLELY IN MADAGASCAR,** the ring-tailed lemur sleeps for about 16 hours a day! Lemurs like to sleep in groups, all clumped together. During their waking hours they spend a lot of time on the ground, a behavior that sets them apart from most other tree-dwelling lemurs.

# L is for
## Lazy

## Sloth ⟶

**SLOTHS ARE THE** definition of slow—their name actually means "reluctance to work or make an effort." But there's a scientific reason behind their sluggishness. Most scientists believe in order to go unnoticed by predators, sloths developed the ability to move in slow-mo!

Sloths travel only 41 yards a day. That's about half the length of a football field! It's also slow enough for algae to grow on their fur while they're hanging from trees. This is actually beneficial to sloths, as they can use it for camouflage in the trees and to feed their young.

# Owl Monkey

**NAMED BECAUSE** of their extraordinarily large eyes, the owl monkey is the only nocturnal monkey. Unlike many other primates, it can't see in color but instead has fantastic night vision. Native to South America, the owl monkey spends 17 hours of its day asleep!

# Opossum

**RATHER THAN SPENDING** time hunting for food, the opossum prefers to scavenge or feed on roadkill. Even when presented with a threat, like a predator, they just play dead instead of attempting to run. They spend 18 to 20 hours of their day snoozing!

# M is for Migration

**THE EARTH'S RESOURCES** ebb and flow depending on the season, so these creatures walk, swim and fly incredible distances to access food, shelter or a good place to raise young.

## Bighorn Sheep

**THE BIGHORN SHEEP** lives up high in the Rocky Mountains, ranging anywhere from Canada to New Mexico! But during the winter months their usual diet of plants becomes scarce, causing these majestic sheep to leave their high-altitude mountain ranges for lower-elevation pastures.

## Sooty Shearwater

**IN JUST ONE YEAR,** the sooty shearwater travels more than most people do in their entire lives. These amazing birds fly from New Zealand to the Northern Pacific Ocean, near California, Alaska and even Japan. This trip totals 40,000 miles!

THE BIGHORN SHEEP'S HORNS ARE A LOT HEAVIER THAN THEY LOOK! THEIR HORNS WEIGH 30 POUNDS! DURING MATING SEASON, MALES FIGHT OVER FEMALES WITH HEAD-BUTTING CONTESTS, CHARGING AT OPPONENTS AT 20 MPH!

# Cownose Ray

**RAYS ARE ONE** of the few animals that migrate by the masses—sometimes their numbers reach 10,000! Cownose rays live all along the Atlantic Coast, from New England to Brazil. They migrate to Chesapeake Bay's shallow waters each summer to give birth.

SOOTY SHEARWATERS FEED ON FISH, SMALL CRUSTACEANS, SQUID AND JELLYFISH!

# M is for Migration

SALMON ARE ANADROMOUS (AH-NAH-DROH-MUSS) FISH. THAT MEANS THEY WERE BORN IN FRESHWATER, BUT GROW UP TO BE SALTWATER FISH. SALMON ONLY RETURN TO THE FRESHWATER TO REPRODUCE.

THIS MIGRATION IS CALLED A SALMON RUN!

## Salmon

**THESE FISH HAVE** one of the most famous migrations. Salmon will swim against the current and jump up waterfalls to return to their breeding grounds. Brown bears in particular love this time of year, as the salmon leaping out of the water are easy to snatch up.

## Canadian Goose

**IN THE COLDER** fall months, geese will leave the northern parts of America and Canada in favor of the balmy American South. Geese stay down there for the winter and fly back up north in the spring!

Geese fly in a V-formation and take turns being the leader. This reduces wind resistance for the birds toward the back, helping all the geese conserve energy over a long flight.

# Moose

**THIS LARGE, ANTLERED** herbivore journeys north in the summer to take advantage of the melted ice and snow in the northern regions of Europe, America and Asia. Moose enjoy the plentiful aquatic plants in the newly thawed lakes, feeding both at and below the surface.

STANDING AT MORE THAN 6 FEET TALL AND WEIGHING ABOUT 1,800 POUNDS, MOOSE ARE SURPRISINGLY GOOD SWIMMERS! THEY CAN SWIM SEVERAL MILES AT A TIME AND EVEN PUT THEIR HEADS UNDERWATER.

## Monarch Butterfly

**NORTH AMERICAN MONARCHS** are the only butterflies that travel up to 3,000 miles each year, heading for the warm weather in California and Mexico. They must begin their journey in the fall, as they can't survive the cold winters east of the Rocky Mountains.

MANATEES USUALLY SWIM AT A STEADY PACE OF 5 MILES PER HOUR, BUT THEY ARE CAPABLE OF SOME BRIEF SPEEDINESS. IN SHORT BURSTS, THEY CAN SWIM UP TO 15 MILES PER HOUR.

## Manatee

**OFTEN REFERRED TO AS** "sea cows," manatees are large water mammals typically found in rivers, canals, coastal areas and saltwater bays. A low metabolic rate means manatees can't survive in the cold, so they head to Florida's warm waters each winter. The Columbus Zoo is proud to be one of the facilities outside of Florida to rehabilitate manatees affected by boat strikes and cold stress.

# Bobolink

**THE BOBOLINK TRAVELS** more than 12,000 miles round trip each year, migrating to South America for the winter and returning to North America for nesting. In order to make such a long journey, scientists believe bobolinks use the magnetic fields of the earth and the position of the stars for navigation.

Although the male bobolink has striking white and black plumage, he doesn't keep this coat year-round. At the end of summer, he sheds these feathers for a brown coat.

# Aardvark

**ALSO CALLED ANTBEARS,** these nocturnal creatures live south of the Sahara in Africa. They spend their afternoons in cool underground burrows and emerge at night to search for termite mounds. Aardvarks claw into the mounds and use their long, sticky tongues to snatch up as many insects as possible.

# Barn Owl

**BARN OWLS CAN** be found all over the world, but you'll probably only see them at night! During the day, they roost in hidden, quiet places. Barn owls like to hunt over large areas of open land, like fields, grasslands and marshes.

# N is for Nocturnal

**WHILE MANY ANIMALS** are diurnal, meaning they are awake during the day, some—including mammals, birds and crustaceans—are nocturnal, which means they are active at night.

## Indian Flying Fox

**WITH AN AVERAGE** wingspan of 4–5 feet, the Indian Flying Fox is a fairly large bat. But don't be alarmed if you see one; these guys only feed on fruit! They'll travel up to 40 miles to find figs, guavas, mangoes and bananas.

Not all bats are "blind!" While insect-feeding bats use echolocation, the Indian flying fox has great night vision.

# N is for **Nocturnal**

**AYE-AYES** ARE THE ONLY PRIMATES THOUGHT TO USE ECHOLOCATION FOR HUNTING!

## Aye-Aye

**THESE WILD-EYED** mammals are found only on the island of Madagascar and are members of the primate family. Aye-ayes have pointed claws on all their digits except for their opposable big toes, which makes them particularly well-suited for spending most of their time in tree branches.

# Lobster

**LOBSTERS ARE EVERYWHERE:** They can be found in all of the world's oceans, in freshwater or places in between. These crustaceans have very poor eyesight, but they make up for it with sense organs on their legs! This helps them detect food as they walk along the sea floor at night.

# Fennec Fox

**THIS PARTICULAR SPECIES** of fox has gained some notoriety because of its giant ears. But these ears are more than just cute: They allow this desert dweller to help stay cool by radiating body heat. Being nocturnal is an advantage in the desert as well—instead of hunting while the sun is out, they are asleep in underground dens!

# N is for
## Nocturnal

## Jerboa

**THIS TINY DESERT** rodent only weighs a few ounces but moves surprisingly fast—up to 16 miles per hour when jumping! The jerboa has excellent dim-light vision to aid it in finding plants, seeds and insects to munch on.

**JERBOAS NEVER NEED TO DRINK WATER!** THEY GET ALL THE HYDRATION THEY NEED FROM THE REST OF THEIR DIET.

## Kinkajou

**THIS SMALL MAMMAL** is closely related to the raccoon and primarily found in Central and South America. They spend much of their time in trees and have feet that can turn backward, enabling them to run in either direction along tree branches and trunks.

# Hippopotamus

**HIPPOS AVOID OVERHEATING** in the African sun by spending up to 16 hours a day in lakes and rivers and secreting a red oily substance that acts as sunblock. When the sun sets, they'll come ashore and walk for miles to eat around 80 pounds of grass.

# O is for Omnivorous

**SOME ANIMALS, LIKE LIONS,** are carnivores and only eat other animals, and some animals, like cows, are herbivores and only eat plants. "Omni" means everything, so omnivores eat both! Chances are you are one!

## Chipmunk

**THIS TINY MEMBER** of the squirrel family is known for its stripes, pudgy cheeks and bushy tails. Those cheeks serve an important purpose: Storing lots of food to bring back to a nest or burrow. Chipmunks feed on nuts, seeds, fruit, grains and insects.

## Maned Wolf

**NATIVE TO SOUTH AMERICA,** the maned wolf has long, spindly legs and a distinctive black strip of fur between the back of its head and shoulders. While the maned wolf eats a wide variety of food, including small mammals, deer, insects, reptiles and fish, the bulk of its diet is made up of the tomato-like lobeira fruit.

# Raccoon

**RACCOONS ARE EASILY** identified by their bandit-like facial markings and the overturned trash cans they leave in their wake! Raccoons eat all sorts of things, including crayfish, frogs, mice, insects, fruit, plants and whatever leftovers they can find in the garbage.

**DURING THE WINTER,** RACCOONS GO INTO A QUASI-HIBERATION. THEY SLEEP A LOT MORE AND LIVE OFF STORED FAT. THEY USUALLY LOSE HALF OF THEIR BODY WEIGHT!

# O is for **Omnivorous**

**WOODPECKERS DON'T ONLY PECK TO SEEK OUT FOOD!** THEY HAVE OTHER REASONS FOR CAUSING SUCH A RACKET. WOODPECKERS ALSO MAKE THOSE ECHOING BEAK-ON-WOOD NOISES TO ATTRACT MATES AND TO ESTABLISH TERRITORY BOUNDARIES. USUALLY ONLY ONE PAIR OF WOODPECKERS WILL LIVE IN A TERRITORY.

## Pileated Woodpecker

**A PILEATED WOODPECKER** will eat fruit and nuts, but its favorite treat is carpenter ants. As their name suggests, woodpeckers use their sharp beaks to peel away bark and dig holes into trees, revealing some tasty insects.

# Woolly Monkey

**NAMED FOR ITS DENSE,** woolly fur, the woolly monkey spends most of its time in the trees of South America. This stocky primate loves eating fruit, but it will also snack on nuts, seeds, leaves, nectar, insects and even small rodents and reptiles.

# Skunk

**SKUNKS ARE RECOGNIZED** by their black and white fur and avoided because of their infamously smelly spray with a 10-foot range. The small North American mammal feasts on fruit, plants, insects, larvae, worms, eggs, reptiles, small mammals and fish.

# O is for **Omnivorous**

## Coati

**CLOSELY RELATED TO RACCOONS,** the cute coati from South America spends most of its time hanging out in trees and searching for insects, fruit, rodents, lizards and snakes to snack on. At night, coatis sleep in treetop nests made from twigs and leaves.

## Cassowary

**THE CASSOWARY IS** a large, flightless bird found in Australia, New Guinea and surrounding islands. Though cassowaries will eat small mammals, reptiles and fish, they are primarily frugivores, meaning they eat mostly fruit.

Because cassowaries have short digestive tracts, a lot of fruit seeds pass through their systems without being digested. For some plants, this process actually helps them sprout more easily!

# Piranha

**FAMOUS FOR THEIR RAZOR-SHARP** teeth and frenzied group feasts, most people probably think piranhas only eat meat. But many species of this South American river fish eat whatever they can find, including aquatic plants, fish, snails, insects and even mammals and birds that fall in the water.

# Jaguar

**THE NAME JAGUAR** is derived from the Native American word *yaguar*, which means "he who kills with one leap." It's an apt name for a big cat that likes to climb trees and wait for an animal to pass by, allowing the jaguar to jump down and snag dinner with one bite.

# Fossa

**THE FOSSA IS** the largest carnivore in Madagascar, making it a fearsome predator to all the other animals on the island. Armed with catlike teeth and retractable claws, the fossa prowls day and night, moving easily among tree branches and on land.

UNLIKE MOST CATS, JAGUARS LOVE WATER! THEY SPEND MOST OF THEIR TIME HUNTING AQUATIC REPTILES.

# P is for **Predators**

**WHILE THEIR EXACT** diets may differ, these hunters have one thing in common—they eat other animals! And because feeding on flesh is no easy feat, these carnivores are highly skilled at catching prey.

## Nile Crocodile

**THESE REPTILIAN PREDATORS** look for prey by keeping only their eyes and nostrils above the water. Nile crocodiles often eat small fish, but with some patience, they can feast on much larger meals, like hippos and zebras.

Within their massive jaws, Nile crocodiles typically have between 64 and 68 cone-shaped teeth.

# P is for Predators

## Ladybug ⟶

**WHILE LADYBUGS LOOK** pretty harmless to humans, they're an aphid's worst enemy! Farmers love ladybugs and their endless appetite for the smaller bugs that like to eat crops. Ladybugs also have the ability to secrete a foul-tasting liquid from their joints, making them unappetizing to predators.

THE STICKY GLUE THIS FROG SECRETES ACTUALLY HAS TWO PURPOSES! NOT ONLY DOES IT PROVIDE FAST FOOD, THE GLUE KEEPS A HUNGRY PREDATOR FROM EATING IT, AND TEMPORARILY GLUES ITS MOUTH SHUT.

## Crucifix Toad →

**NATIVE TO AUSTRALIA,** the crucifix toad is actually a frog with a striking pattern on its back. This frog secretes a very sticky substance from its skin, which ants and termites will get stuck in. When the frog sheds its skin, it eats the whole thing!

THESE LIZARDS CAN RUN ACROSS ABOUT 5 FEET OF WATER!

## Green Basilisk Lizard

**THIS SMALL LIZARD** might not look intimidating, but it has a very special skill. This lizard's quick speed and specially designed feet allow it to run on water, making it especially deadly to insects.

# **P** is for **Predators**

## Trapdoor Spider

**DESPITE ITS SMALL STATURE,** the trapdoor spider manages to have a diverse diet of animals. This spider lives up to its name by waiting in a small burrow to attack and consume any insects or small animals that come near. Among its prey are baby snakes, frogs and small fish.

In ecology, the relationship between predators and their prey is called predation. Some predators will kill their prey and then eat it later, while others attack and kill prey in the process of eating it.

# Long-Tailed Weasel

**SIZE DOESN'T MEAN** much to the long-tailed weasel, a vicious carnivore known to feast on much larger animals. Chipmunks, tree squirrels, shrews and moles are among the preferred foods of these rodents. But if they can't find a small mammal to make a meal of, long-tailed weasels will eat insects, frogs and bird eggs instead.

# Grasshopper Mouse

**NOT ALL CARNIVORES** are massive and mighty—some are small, like the grasshopper mouse. Known to be quite stealthy stalkers, these little rodents will hunt and kill small animals like worms, scorpions and snakes. Grasshopper mice even eat fellow rodents such as kangaroo rats on occasion.

# Q is for Quick

**WHETHER AN ANIMAL** is trying to catch its own dinner or avoid becoming someone else's, it's useful to be fast in the wild!

## Mexican Free-Tailed Bat

**A GROUP OF BATS** is known as a colony, and the Mexican free-tailed bat usually travels in colonies made up of several million bats! They are extremely fast, traveling up to 47 miles per hour in open spaces.

**MEXICAN FREE-TAILED BATS HAVE** LONG HAIRS ON THEIR TOES TO HELP JUDGE FLIGHT SPEED AND TURBULENCE!

## Sailfish

**NAMED FOR THEIR** sail-like dorsal fins, sailfish are found in the warmer parts of the sea. They're the fastest fish in the ocean, having been recorded jumping out of the water at more than 68 miles per hour.

# Peregrine Falcon

**PEREGRINE FALCONS** are known for their incredible speed and skill at catching prey in mid-flight. When a peregrine falcon dives, it can hit speeds of more than 200 miles per hour!

Peregrine falcons that nest in the Arctic tundra but spend their winters in South America fly up to 15,500 miles in one year!

# Q is for **Quick**

**IT'S ONLY FEMALE HORSEFLIES THAT BITE!** MALE HORSEFLIES FEED ON POLLEN AND NECTAR.

## Horsefly

**THESE INSECTS ARE KNOWN** for being very loud pests with a nasty bite. But they're also stupendously fast fliers—they have a top speed of 90 miles per hour!

# Frigatebird

**THE FRIGATEBIRD** has amazing speed and endurance. This tropical seabird has an impressive top speed of 95 miles per hour, and takes advantage of updrafts to remain soaring for weeks at a time! They feed during these long trips by stealing food from other birds or snatching small fish jumping out of the water.

The brown hare is mostly nocturnal! They spend most of the day in small depressions in the grass called "forms," and venture out at night to graze on grass and crops.

# Brown Hare

**THE BROWN HARE** is found all over western and central Europe, including most of the United Kingdom. Its powerful hind legs allow the hare to reach speeds of up to 45 miles per hour!

# Q is for Quick

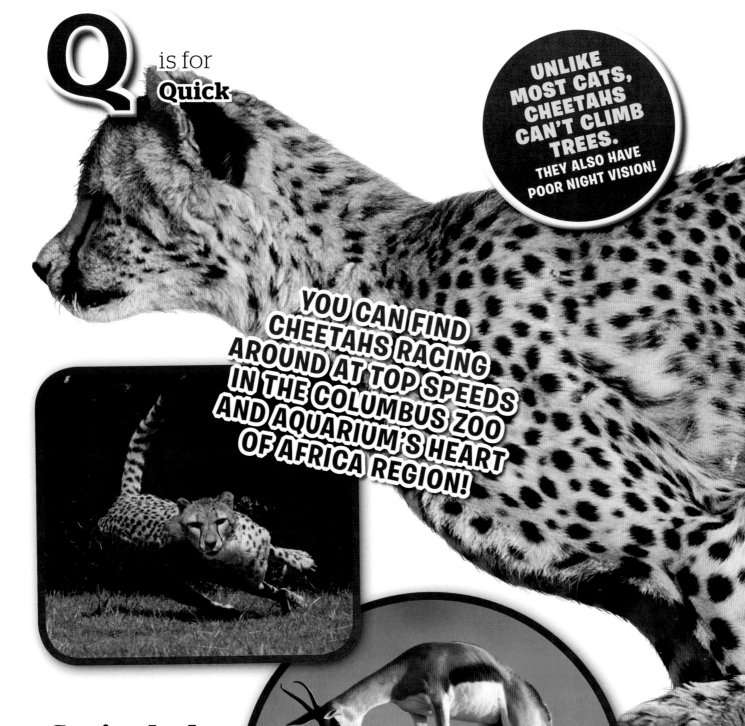

**UNLIKE MOST CATS, CHEETAHS CAN'T CLIMB TREES.** THEY ALSO HAVE POOR NIGHT VISION!

YOU CAN FIND CHEETAHS RACING AROUND AT TOP SPEEDS IN THE COLUMBUS ZOO AND AQUARIUM'S HEART OF AFRICA REGION!

## Springbok →

**CLOSELY RELATED TO** the gazelle, the springbok is one of the 10 fastest animals on land. When they're not jumping in the air (also called pronking), this African grazer can run up to 56 miles per hour!

## Cheetah

**CHEETAHS ARE THE FASTEST** animals on land, with the ability to go from 0 to 60 miles per hour in just three seconds. However, as cheetahs can't keep their speed up for very long, most hunts are over in under a minute.

## Swordfish

**SWORDFISH SECRETE AN OIL** from the base of their bill, creating a water-repelling layer across the front of its head. This lets the swordfish travel through water with less resistance and reach speeds of more than 60 miles per hour!

# R is for **Rodents**

**RODENTS ARE CHARACTERIZED** by the long, sharp teeth they use for gnawing. They're found all over the world, making up more than half of the world's mammals.

## Chinchilla

**WITH THEIR FURRY** faces and silky fur, chinchillas make for popular pets. Owners must buy volcanic ash so their chinchillas can take dust baths at least once a week. They are extremely social and live in colonies with hundreds of other chinchillas in the wild.

**CHINCHILLAS WERE ALMOST HUNTED TO EXTINCTION** BECAUSE OF INTEREST IN THEIR SOFT FUR. HOWEVER, THANKS TO HUNTING BANS, THE CHINCHILLA POPULATION IS UP AGAIN IN SOUTH AMERICA.

## Rat

**THOUGH THERE ARE** 56 different species of rats, the two best-known to humans are the brown rat and the house rat, as these two species are found everywhere humans are. The brown rat's dense fur makes it particularly adept at swimming and hunting for food in lakes, streams and sewers, while the house rat has superior climbing abilities.

# Beaver

**THESE CUTE AND CUDDLY** looking critters are the largest rodents in North America. But unlike most other members of the rodent family, they spend a great deal of time underwater. Beavers can swim underwater for up to 15 minutes at a time, and they even have see-through eyelids! This allows them to see clearly while still keeping water out of their eyes.

BEAVERS HAVE OILY, WATERPROOF FUR!

# R is for Rodents

**DEGUS WORK AS A TEAM AND FORM ELABORATE DIGGING CHAINS!** THE FIRST DEGUS IN THE CHAIN DO THE DIGGING AND THEN THE LOOSE DIRT IS PASSED DOWN THE CHAIN UNTIL IT'S OUT OF THE BURROW ENTIRELY.

## Degu

**THIS SMALL,** rat-like rodent is one of the most common mammals in central Chile, often found on the lower slopes of the Andes Mountains. Degus live in large colonies and excavate elaborate underground systems made up of several main chambers with interconnecting tunnels.

# Groundhog

**ALSO KNOWN AS** woodchucks, groundhogs are the largest members of the squirrel family. Though they spend most of their time on the ground, they are also adept at climbing trees and swimming. Groundhogs eat as much as they can during the summer so they can live off their fat stores while hibernating through much of the winter.

# Paca

**THESE RODENTS ARE FOUND** in the tropical forests of Latin America, often near sources of water. The nocturnal pacas spend their nights loudly foraging for fruit, plants and tubers. If threatened, a paca will retreat to the water—they're very good swimmers!

A paca can stay submerged under water for up to 15 minutes! By that point, predators have moved on.

# R is for Rodents

## Capybara

**RANGING FROM 60** to a whopping 174 pounds, capybaras are the largest rodents on earth. Nicknamed "water pigs," capybaras have slightly webbed feet and can often be found in riverbanks, marshes and ponds, grazing on aquatic plants and grasses.

## Mara

**ALSO KNOWN AS** a Patagonian mara, this rodent looks like a cross between a deer and a rabbit. Unlike most mammals, maras are strictly monogamous, meaning they mate for life. Once mated, maras rarely interact with other members of their own species.

# Porcupine

**THIS RODENT IS** famous for being particularly prickly—they have more than 30,000 quills! Though porcupines cannot shoot these quills at predators, they do come detached very easily. Any animal that tangles with a porcupine has a good chance of leaving with quills in its face or body.

# S
## is for **Spots**

**WHILE SOME ANIMALS'** spots are great for camouflage, scientists don't always know why other animals have them. They're really neat to look at, though!

## Ocelot

**OCELOTS ARE NOCTURNAL,** spotted cats that mostly live in South American rainforests. They're excellent predators that hunt rabbits, rodents, iguanas, fish and frogs. They even climb trees in search of monkeys and birds. Because their teeth aren't suited for chewing, ocelots tear their food into small pieces and swallow them whole.

# Dalmatian

**THE DALMATIAN'S SPOTTED** coat and reputation as a firehouse dog has made it one of the best-recognized dog breeds. As pups, dalmatians have pure white coats and usually develop their spots by about four weeks.

# Whale Shark

**WHALE SHARKS ARE** dotted sharks, not whales. They got their name by being the largest fish in the sea! The largest whale shark ever seen was 40 feet long, but scientists believe they can grow even larger. This shark populates all tropical seas, and feeds by simply opening its jaw and filtering everything that passes into its mouth. As a result, the whale shark eats a lot of plankton and small fish.

Whale sharks serve as the ocean's public transportation, allowing some fish to swim along on their backs.

## S

is for **Spots**

## Appaloosa

**THE APPALOOSA IS** slightly larger than the average horse and is prized for its dappled coat and striped hooves. It's a multi-talented breed well-suited for riding, jumping, racing and work.

UNLIKE MOST OTHER HORSES, THE APPALOOSA HAS SCLERA, BETTER KNOWN AS THE WHITES OF EYES. THIS HORSE ALSO MOLTS, SHEDDING THE SKIN OF ITS FACE AND SNOUT.

# Pietrain Pig

**PIETRAIN PIGS ARE** a breed of domestic pig from Belgium that have become very popular in other countries, especially Germany. They're shorter and stockier than most domestic pigs, with distinct, piebald markings on their coats.

# Spotted Trunkfish

**THE SPOTTED TRUNKFISH** has a bony structure and sharp spines guarding their rear fins, which combined act as a sort of built-in body armor. This is good news for them, as they're not very strong swimmers. The spotted trunkfish feeds on a wide variety of foods, including mollusks, crustaceans, sea plants and algae.

## S is for **Spots**

# Spotted Bush Snake

**THE SPOTTED BUSH** snake is found in the northern regions of Africa and feeds on geckos, chameleons and tree frogs. Its bright to olive green body is sprinkled with dark spots, allowing it to blend into the shadows of greenery.

# Spotted Moray Eel

**MORAYS MAKE THEMSELVES** at home in rock crevices along the bottom of the sea. These spotted predators have been found at depths of up to 656 feet, and use their sharp teeth to snatch up smaller fish, mollusks and crustaceans.

BRIGHT YELLOW WITH BLACK SPLOTCHES, THE TURTLE'S UNDERBELLY GETS DARKER AS IT BECOMES OLDER.

# Spotted Turtle

**AT JUST OVER** 5 inches long, spotted turtles are rather small reptiles that look as though someone splattered them with paint! They're found primarily along the eastern seaboard and Great Lakes region of North America and have extremely long lifespans, with males living up to 65 years and females living to be 110.

# T is for Tentacles

**TENTACLES ARE** flexible, long organs, often used for grasping, feeding and getting around.

## Jellyfish

**THESE SEA CREATURES** use their tentacles as weapons! They're filled with tiny stinging cells that paralyze their prey. Jellyfish prey on fish, shrimp and tiny crabs, but they will also eat plants.

**LOTS OF JELLYFISH ARE CLEAR, BUT THEY CAN ALSO BE PINK, YELLOW, BLUE OR PURPLE. THEY ALSO TEND TO BE BIOLUMINESCENT, MEANING THEY CAN PRODUCE LIGHT!**

# Giant Squid →

**THESE TENTACLED HUNTERS** can catch fish up to 33 feet away. The ends of their tentacles are tipped with hundreds of sharp toothed suckers, perfect for drawing in prey. Giant squids also boast the largest eyes in the animal kingdom—they're the size of dinner plates!

# Snail

**MOST SNAILS HAVE** two sets of tentacles that function as sensory organs. The upper pair has their eyes, while the lower pair lets them smell. But don't bother yelling at a snail: They don't have ears to hear!

**T** is for **Tentacles**

# Sea Anemone

**THESE INVERTEBRATES** may look like plants, but they're actually animals that are closely related to jellyfish. If a fish swims too close and brushes up against its tentacles, the sea anemone injects a paralyzing venom and traps it for lunch.

There are more than 1,000 species of anemones! They can be as short as half an inch or as long as 6 feet!

# Cuttlefish

**THIS MOLLUSK'S TENTACLES** are located around its mouth, helping it to catch prey and quickly eat it. A cuttlefish also has the ability to change color, enabling it to camouflage itself while waiting to snatch up a crustacean or fish.

# Banana Slug

**COUSIN TO THE SNAIL,** banana slugs also have two pairs of tentacles, with the upper pair holding their eyes and the lower pair allowing them to smell and feel. The slug's mouth is located between the lower two tentacles and contains a radula, a tongue-like organ covered in tiny teeth.

# T is for Tentacles

## Star-Nosed Mole

**THIS PECULIAR LOOKING** mammal has a hairless nose with 22 fleshy pink tentacles. The tentacles are immensely useful sensory organs, with the ability to identify prey in under half a second while foraging. This is especially useful for the star-nosed mole, which roots around in dirt looking for worms, larvae and insects to snack on.

This mole has 30,000 touch fibers in its snout, while the entire human hand only has 17,000!

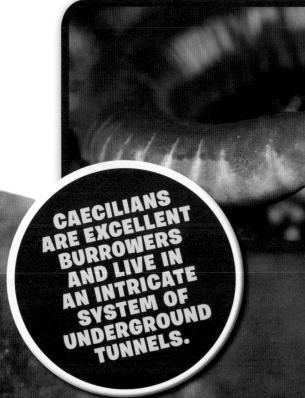

# Caecilian

**THIS ANIMAL LOOKS** similar to a worm, but it's actually a legless amphibian. Caecilians are the only amphibians to possess tentacles: They have a very small pair of sensory tentacles located between their nose and eyes.

CAECILIANS ARE EXCELLENT BURROWERS AND LIVE IN AN INTRICATE SYSTEM OF UNDERGROUND TUNNELS.

## Coral

**SINGLE CORAL ORGANISMS** can live on their own, but coral famously constructs large communities known as reefs. Coral can live for centuries, mostly feeding off the byproducts of the algae that lives on them. To supplement their diet, coral also has barbed, venomous tentacles for grabbing zooplankton and small fish.

# U

## is for
# Ursine

**URSINE MEANS BEAR-LIKE!** Bears are large mammals found in North and South America, Europe and Asia.

### Grizzly Bear

**BEING AS BIG** as they are, grizzly bears require fairly massive meals. But while they are great hunters and famously catch salmon, this subspecies of brown bear has a diet mostly made up of fruit, nuts, leaves and roots! In 2004, two Alaskan brown bear orphans were rescued and brought to the Columbus Zoo and Aquarium. I love watching Brutus and Buckeye grow—both in size and maturity!

# Sun Bear

**WEIGHING ONLY** 60 to 150 pounds, sun bears are the smallest species of bear. Native to Southeast Asia, sun bears have extra long tongues that are extremely useful for getting honey out of beehives. They also have long claws, which they use for ripping into termite nests.

# Spectacled Bear

**NAMED FOR THEIR** distinctive facial markings, the spectacled bear lives in the Andean jungles of South America. While they occasionally eat rodents, birds, insects and even small cows, spectacled bears are mostly vegetarian. They are extremely agile climbers and have been known to sit in trees for days waiting for fruit to ripen.

Similar to human fingerprints, spectacled bears all have unique facial, neck and chest markings. Scientists believe there are only 3,000 of these bears left, though, because of the destruction of their habitat.

# U is for **Ursine**

← **Polar Bear**

**POLAR BEARS ARE** found in the Arctic, where they spend most of their time hunting seals. These bears like to wait at holes in the ice for a seal to come up for breath, but they can also hunt by swimming beneath the ice.

## Gobi Bear

**A KIND OF BROWN BEAR** native to the Gobi Desert, the Gobi bear is extremely endangered, with only a few dozen left. The Gobi bear has longer limbs and a shorter coat than most brown bears and feeds on plants, insects and lizards.

# Black Bear

**BLACK BEARS ARE** the most common bears in North America, and can have coats in many different colors, including gray, brown, cinnamon and even white. Black bears are excellent climbers thanks to their short claws—some black bears even decide to spend the winter in a tree hole, instead of building a den in a cave or burrow.

AT 4.5 FEET LONG, BLACK BEARS ARE AMERICA'S SMALLEST BEARS.

# U is for Ursine

IN JUST ONE DAY, A GIANT PANDA WILL EAT ANYWHERE FROM 26 TO 84 POUNDS OF BAMBOO! LUCKILY, THEY'RE GREAT TREE CLIMBERS AND CAN USE THEIR ENLARGED WRISTS TO GATHER THE FOOD THEY NEED.

## Giant Panda

**BELOVED FOR ITS BEAUTIFUL** black and white coat, the giant panda is perhaps the most famously endangered species in the world. Their current population in the wilderness of China is just more than 1,800. Giant pandas are exclusive to the Asian country, feeding off the forests of bamboo found there.

# Kodiak Bear

**ONLY FOUND ON** the islands of the Kodiak Archipelago, these bears are a subspecies of brown bears. Kodiak bears have been isolated from other bears on these islands for more than 10,000 years! Fortunately, the area has plenty of salmon, berries and seaweed for them to eat.

THE SLOTH BEAR IS THE ONLY KIND OF BEAR TO CARRY ITS YOUNG ON ITS BACK.

# Sloth Bear

**FOUND IN SOUTH ASIA,** the sloth bear's favorite foods are termites and ants. The black furry bear uses its long claws to break nest mounds, then sucks up any tasty insects inside through a gap in its front teeth.

# V is for Venomous

**ANIMALS CAPABLE OF** delivering venom can come in all shapes and sizes. In some cases, venom is used by an animal to capture its prey. But for many, the use of venom is a means of protection against predators.

> While stonefish look immobile, they can be very fast. When prey is around, a high-speed camera is needed to capture the hunt!

## Stonefish

**THE STONEFISH IS** the most venomous fish in the world! It has a venomous sac on each of its 13 spines. The venom is a defense mechanism: It's emitted when a predator attacks or when an unsuspecting human steps on the stonefish, thinking it's just a rock.

## Wasp

**NOT ALL VARIETIES OF** wasps are venomous, but the ones that sting certainly are! Some wasps use their stingers only defensively, while others use them to attack their prey. Unlike bees, wasps can use their stingers multiple times.

## Cone Snail

**AS THE MOST VENOMOUS SNAIL** in the deep blue sea, an encounter with the marbled cone snail often results in death. Injecting the venom via a tooth that shoots out like a harpoon, the cone snail kills their would-be predators instantly.

# V is for **Venomous**

## Blue-Ringed Octopus

**THE BLUE-RINGED OCTOPUS** only weighs about two ounces, but don't let this tiny cephalopod trick you into thinking it's harmless—its venom is more toxic than any land animal's. In fact, this octopus has two types of venom. One is used for hunting crabs, while the second, more toxic venom is used for defending against predators.

The black mamba can grow to be as long as 14 feet! That's longer than an elephant is tall!

# Black Mamba

**THE BLACK MAMBA** is one of the fastest snakes in the world, slithering at up to 12.5 miles per hour. A bite from a black mamba snake is deadly, often killing prey or predators within 20 minutes.

**SLOW LORISES ARE THE ONLY POISONOUS PRIMATES IN THE WORLD!**

# Slow Loris

**THEY MAY APPEAR** cute and cuddly, but slow lorises are capable of being very dangerous if attacked. If this primate is threatened, it licks its elbows to extract a venom from its glands. With the venom stored in its saliva, the slow loris then bites the predator, filling the wound with the toxic fluid.

## is for **Venomous**

# Brown Recluse Spider

**THIS SPIDER LIVES** in the middle of America. As its name suggests, it would much rather flee than fight when confronted with another predator or human. When brown recluse spiders must fight, they take a big bite and inject venom into whatever is attacking them. The venom kills other insects and can send humans to the hospital!

**ONLY THIS NEWT AND SEVERAL TYPES OF SALAMANDERS USE THEIR RIBS AS SPEARS.**

# Iberian Ribbed Newt

**BY THRUSTING OUT** their rib bones through their own skin, the Iberian ribbed newt is able to create sharp, venomous weapons that are sure to ward off any predator! They're also great hunters in their own right, eating any moving prey they find.

# Indian Red Scorpion

**THIS TINY ARACHNID** is known as the world's deadliest scorpion. Most commonly found in India, Pakistan and Nepal, their stingers contain an extremely powerful venom that's useful for both capturing prey and defending themselves against larger predators.

There are almost 2,000 species of scorpion, but not all of them are venomous. Thick-tailed scorpions with small pincers have venom in their stingers, while thin-tailed ones with large pincers do not.

# W

## is for
## Web-Footed

**PART FOOT, PART FIN,** webbed feet give these animals the best of both worlds! Webbed feet allow animals to move more easily in water, while still letting them walk on land.

## Trumpeter Swan

**SWANS ARE THE** fastest species of waterfowl, both in the water and in the air. These birds are known for swimming, flying and even eating in a graceful manner. Instead of diving for food as most waterfowl do, swans dabble: They stand in shallow waters and pick at aquatic plants.

# Spot-Billed Duck

**THOUGH THEY WADDLE ON LAND PRETTY WELL,** ducks are made for swimming. Their webbed-feet act as paddles, enabling them to move easily through the water. Also, all ducks have waterproof outer feathers, letting them dive deep underwater without their underlayer getting wet. Because of this, ducks can tolerate extremely cold water.

# Flat-Headed Cat →

**THIS UNUSUAL CAT** from South East Asia has a special advantage when it comes to hunting fish: partially webbed feet! The flat-headed cat also has a long jaw and sharp, backward-pointing teeth to help catch and keep slippery fish.

# W

is for **Web-Footed**

## Muskrat

**LIKE THEIR BEAVER RELATIVES,** muskrats are semi-aquatic mammals that are great builders. For shelter, muskrats either construct lodges out of vegetation and mud or dig underwater tunnels that lead out to a place above water level. Because of their hind-webbed feet, muskrats are great swimmers and enjoy a diet of many small aquatic animals and plants.

**OTTERS LIKE TO BUILD BURROWS NEAR THE EDGE OF THE WATER** AND MAKE TUNNELS LEADING TO THE RIVER. THIS LETS THEM COME AND GO FROM THE WATER AS THEY PLEASE!

## North American River Otter

**THOUGH THEY CAN RUN** quite well on land, otters really belong in the water. Otters are wonderful swimmers, thanks to their long bodies, powerful tails, webbed feet and water-repellent fur. On top of all this, their nostrils and ears close when they're underwater, and they can hold their breath for about eight minutes!

# Flamingo →

**THESE BIRDS ARE SURPRISINGLY** good swimmers, but they spend most of their time feeding in mud flats. Flamingos use their webbed feet to stir up the mud and water, then stick their beaks (and sometimes their whole head!) in the ground to suck up any tasty plankton, tiny fish or fly larvae. Their beaks have special filters to separate food from water, allowing them to only ingest what they need and spit the rest back out.

FLAMINGOS GET THEIR BRIGHT PINK COLOR BY EATING LOTS OF SHRIMPLIKE CRUSTACEANS! IF THIS IS LACKING IN THEIR DIET, THEY WILL BECOME PALE.

# W

is for **Web-Footed**

## Albatross

**THE ALBATROSS HAS** a wingspan of up to 11 feet, the longest of any bird. They spend much of their life near the ocean, drinking salt water and primarily dining on squid and schooling fish. The albatross's webbed feet assist them in floating on water, though they tend not to stay for very long, as doing so makes them vulnerable to predators.

## Platypus

**WITH ITS ICONIC LONG BILL,** this aquatic mammal is quite recognizable. The platypus searches for food among the muddy bottoms of rivers, using its bill to detect the likes of insects and small animals. To make this process even more effective, the platypus uses the receptors of its bill to sense electricity.

Did you know male platypuses are venomous? On the heels of their back feet are barbs that can send a toxic blow to any enemy!

# Emperor Penguin

**ONE OF THE FEW** animals to make its home on the icy glaciers of Antarctica, this flightless bird uses its webbed feet to paddle through freezing waters and go fishing. Like all penguins, the emperor penguin is an excellent swimmer, able to stay underwater for up to 20 minutes!

THE AVERAGE EMPEROR PENGUIN IS ALMOST FOUR FEET TALL!

AFTER A MOTHER PENGUIN HAS LAID AN EGG, SHE LEAVES TO GO HUNT FOR HER AND HER UNHATCHED BABY. MEANWHILE, THE FATHER WILL SIT AND KEEP THE EGG WARM FOR TWO MONTHS—WITHOUT FOOD!

# X

## is for
## Xerophilous

**IF A PLANT** or animal is xerophilous (pronounced zero-feel-us), that means it has adapted to a very dry climate or habitat—usually in a really cool way! In other words, all animals that live in deserts are xerophilous.

## Thorny Devil →

**THIS LIZARD'S** spiky structure does more than just encourage predators to think twice about eating it, it also collects water! At night—the spikes on the thorny devil's body collect dew, just as a plant's leaves would. The dew runs down the spikes into small channels on the thorny devil's body, which funnel that water right to its mouth.

## Cactus Ferruginous Pygmy-Owl

**THIS OWL MAKES** the most of its environment by making nests in cacti, often in holes left behind by woodpeckers. Though they're rather small owls, they are impressive hunters, preying on lizards, insects, rodents and even other birds. In fact, a cactus ferruginous pygmy-owl can take down a dove twice its size!

## Camel

**A CAMEL'S HUMP** is filled with fat, not water. Camels can break down this fat into water and energy when other sustenance is not available. That's why they can travel up to 100 miles in the hot desert without drinking!

SUZI AND I LOVE VISITING THE CAMELS THAT ROAM THE 10,000 ACRES AT THE WILDS!

is for
## Xerophilous

## Gila Monster

**THE GILA MONSTER IS** found in the southwestern deserts of the U.S. and the northwestern deserts of Mexico. Scientists think they might spend more than 95 percent of their lives in underground burrows, only coming up to feed and lounge in the sun. Gila monsters store large amounts of fat in their tails, allowing them to go months in between meals.

**GILA MONSTER IS PRONOUNCED HEE-LA MONSTER!**

# Cactus Wren

**THE CACTUS WREN IS** well-adapted to its desert habitat, getting most of the water it needs from its food, which includes insects, fruits, seeds and sometimes small frogs and lizards. It chooses large cacti, thorny plants or strong bushes in which to build its large nests.

# Bobcat

**BOBCATS ARE HIGHLY** adaptable creatures that live just about everywhere in North America, including forests, swamps and deserts. In the desert, bobcats prefer rocky areas with plenty of plant cover. They are able to thrive all over because they'll eat just about anything. A bobcat's favorite meal is rabbit, but they will also eat birds, rodents, snakes, lizards and even the remains of animals other predators have already feasted on.

## is for
## Xerophilous

**SOMETIMES MALE TORTOISES WILL FIGHT FOR DOMINANCE.** THEY FIGHT BY BUMPING THE HORNS ON THEIR SHELLS AGAINST EACH OTHER. THE TORTOISE THAT KNOCKS THE OTHER ONE OVER WINS!

# Desert Tortoise

**TO DEAL WITH LIVING** in the desert, these tortoises both hibernate in burrows during cold months and go dormant during really hot periods, a behavior known as aestivation (ess-tih-vay-shun). When the weather is fair enough for the desert tortoise to be active, it spends a great deal of time munching on desert grasses, which supply it with both sustenance and water.

# Pronghorn

**NEITHER DEER NOR ANTELOPE,** the pronghorn can run an impressive 35 mph for long distances and reach speeds of up to 60 mph for short bursts. The pronghorn is also well-adapted to its desert environment: It can stand temperatures as high as 130 degrees Fahrenheit and as low as 50 below zero!

# Armadillo Lizard

**THIS LIZARD HAS** borrowed the armadillo's ability to roll into a ball when threatened, presenting only spiny scales to any potential predators. The scales also protect the armadillo lizard from its natural habitat, keeping it from sustaining cuts and scratches when scrambling in and out of cracks in rocky outcrops.

The armadillo lizard is one of the few species of reptiles that doesn't lay any eggs! The female lizard will instead give birth to two or three baby lizards.

# Green Grocer Cicada

**CICADAS ARE EXTREMELY** loud bugs, often annoying people with their incessant buzzing and clicking. While it all sounds the same to us, cicadas have different calls for communicating alarm and trying to attract mates. Male cicadas are the ones making all the ruckus by vibrating membranes on their abdomens.

By forgetting where they bury their seeds for winter grub, the red squirrel unintentionally plants a lot of trees!

# Y is for **Yappy**

**WHILE ANIMALS DON'T** have a form of communication as complex as people, they can be extremely chatty in their own ways! These are some of the noisiest animals around.

## Howler Monkey

**LIKE LIONS AND WOLVES,** howler monkeys are also fans of loudly announcing that they've claimed a certain territory. Male howler monkeys in particular have large throats and specialized vocal chambers to help them powerfully cry out—a troop of yelling howler monkeys can be heard up to three miles away.

## Red Squirrel

**WHEN A PREDATOR** approaches the red squirrel's home or nest, the squirrel uses its vocal cords to scare away the unwanted intruder. With a combination of squeals, yips and rattles, the red squirrel sends the trespasser running!

**Y**

is for **Yappy**

## Gray Wolf

**WOLVES USE THEIR** loud howl as a form of communication. Howls from a lone wolf often mean it is seeking attention from its pack, while a group of wolves howling may be alerting others of their territory. Wolves can hear each other up to six miles apart in a forest and up to 10 miles away on tundra.

WHEN A PACK OF WOLVES HOWLS TOGETHER, IT'S CALLED CHORUS HOWLING!

## Lion

**MALE LIONS USE** their impressive roar to help mark their territory. Carrying as far as five miles, the noise both warns potential intruders and helps any straggling members of the pride find their way back home.

## Coqui Frog

**NATIVE TO PUERTO RICO,** the coqui frog is the loudest amphibian in the world. The male's singing can reach about 100 decibels, which is a little louder than the average lawn mover. Pretty impressive for a frog that only weighs up to 4 ounces!

## Y

## is for **Yappy**

# Blue Whale

**KNOWN FOR BEING** the largest animals on the planet, blue whales are also rather talkative. Through various pulses, groans and moans, blue whales can hear each other up to 1,000 miles away! While their noises are likely a form of communication, scientists also believe blue whales make these sounds to sonar-navigate in the darker depths of the ocean.

**BLUE WHALES EAT FOUR TONS OF KRILL A DAY AND CAN EAT THOUSANDS IN ONE BITE!**

# Prairie Dogs →

**THESE CRITTERS ARE** mostly known for creating underground "towns" made of intricate tunnel systems, complete with designated nurseries, sleeping areas and toilets. Because their only defense is hiding, a prairie dog will let out a cry to alert the rest of its town when there is danger. A second "all clear" cry is let out when the predator has passed.

# African Grey Parrot →

**KNOWN FOR THEIR** ability to "talk," some parrots are excellent at imitating human speech. The most skilled mimic is the African grey parrot, which is also known to imitate other animals and bird calls in the wild.

African grey parrots are highly intelligent creatures. Studies have shown they can be taught to use language beyond mimicking, similar to the way apes can learn sign language.

# Z is for **Zombies**

**ZOMBIES ARE REAL!** Well, sort of. In the animal world there are a few different versions of "zombies," from animals that have their minds controlled by parasites to those that can practically come back from the dead!

## Cockroach

**IF A COCKROACH** crosses paths with a pregnant wasp, chances are it's about to become a living incubator. Wasps use their venom to render the cockroach unconscious, then lay their eggs inside them. The cockroach remains alive, protecting the eggs. This provides both a warm place for the eggs to mature as well as a meal for when they hatch!

# South American Fire Ant

**THE SOUTH AMERICAN FIRE ANT** is likely to have a certain species of parasitic fly lay eggs inside its body. After the eggs hatch into larvae, they eat the ant's brain! Scientists think the flies then release chemicals to control the ant's actions. The ant continues to work as usual, but eventually the flies make the ant mindlessly wander to a safe place away from its colony where they can emerge.

# Pill Bug

**PILLS BUGS ARE** vulnerable to parasites that ultimately want to live inside the digestive tract of a bird. To achieve this, the parasite that has grown up inside the pill bug is able to make it stand out in the open, virtually guaranteeing that it will be snatched up by a bird for a snack.

ALTHOUGH "BUG" MIGHT BE IN ITS NAME, THE PILL BUG IS ACTUALLY A VERY SMALL CRUSTACEAN THAT CAN SPEND ALL ITS TIME ON LAND.

# Z is for **Zombies**

## Wood Frog

**WOOD FROGS ARE** perhaps as close as nature gets to the living dead. These frogs are so well-acclimated to cold North American weather that they can almost completely freeze over and hop away afterward! Thanks to a sort of antifreeze in their bloodstream, wood frogs can stand having up to 70 percent of their internal water frozen for up to four weeks.

# Cricket

**ONCE INSIDE A CRICKET,** hairworms produce mind-controlling chemicals that make its host extremely attracted to light. At night, the moonlight reflected off a body of water will draw the cricket right in, despite the fact that crickets drown very easily. This works out very well for the hairworm, which must be in an aquatic habitat in order to reproduce.

**WOOD FROGS ARE THE ONLY FROGS THAT LIVE IN THE ARCTIC CIRCLE!**

# Mud Crab

**PARASITIC BARNACLES ARE** bad news for mud crabs. While this isn't typical barnacle behavior—most prefer to attach themselves to hard objects—some species like to make their homes out of living creatures, especially crabs. If this happens, the crab will lose its reproductive abilities, along with its desire to do anything except be a home to barnacles.

# **Z** is for **Zombies**

## Honeybee

**PARASITIC FLIES LIKE** to lay their eggs in honeybees. As the eggs hatch into grubs, they eat the honeybees from the inside out. Eventually, the flies make the honeybee abandon its hive to find them a safe space to emerge.

Because the caterpillar is trying to reach its cocoon stage, it constantly eats. A caterpillar can grow to be 1,000 times larger than its original size by molting!

## Caterpillar

**THE WASP STRIKES AGAIN!** Wasps may also choose to lay their eggs in baby caterpillars. However, this does not kill them. Once the eggs hatch and wasps emerge, the caterpillar remains oddly loyal to the wasps that previously nested inside, covering them with silk and attempting to protect them from potential predators.

## Killifish

**SIMILAR TO PILL BUGS,** killifish are susceptible to parasites known as flukes that ultimately need to live in a bird's digestive tract. Once inside the killifish, the fluke will release chemicals in the fish's brain, causing it to jump around and attract the attention of hungry sea birds.

# Index

### Aardvark (90)
**LENGTH** 43 to 53 inches
**GROUP** Mammal
**DIET** Omnivore

### African Grey Parrot (161)
**LENGTH** 13 to 16 inches, 18- to 20-inch wingspan
**GROUP** Bird
**DIET** Omnivore

### African Painted Dog (39)
**LENGTH** 30 to 43 inches
**GROUP** Mammal
**DIET** Carnivore

### Albatross (148)
**LENGTH** 3 to 4 feet, 6.5- to 11-foot wingspan
**GROUP** Bird
**DIET** Carnivore

### Alligator (68)
**LENGTH** 10 to 15 feet
**GROUP** Reptile
**DIET** Carnivore

### Alligator Snapping Turtle (70)
**LENGTH** 26 inches
**GROUP** Reptile
**DIET** Carnivore

### Alpaca (35)
**LENGTH** 32 to 38 inches
**GROUP** Mammal
**DIET** Herbivore

### Appaloosa (122)
**HEIGHT** 64 inches
**GROUP** Mammal
**DIET** Herbivore

### Arctic Fox (16)
**LENGTH** 18 to 27 inches
**GROUP** Mammal
**DIET** Omnivore

### Armadillo (78)
**LENGTH** 5 inches to 5 feet
**GROUP** Mammal
**DIET** Omnivore

### Armadillo Lizard (155)
**LENGTH** 3 to 9 inches
**GROUP** Reptile
**DIET** Omnivore

### Assassin Bug (65)
**LENGTH** 0.2 to 1.6 inches
**GROUP** Arthropod
**DIET** Carnivore

### Atlantic Puffin (22)
**LENGTH** 10 inches, 20- to 24-inch wingspan
**GROUP** Bird
**DIET** Carnivore

## Axolotl (38)

**LENGTH** 9 to 12 inches
**GROUP** Amphibian
**DIET** Carnivore

## Aye-Aye (92)

**LENGTH** 14 to 17 inches
**GROUP** Mammal
**DIET** Omnivore

# B

## Babirusa (68)

**LENGTH** 3 feet
**GROUP** Mammal
**DIET** Omnivore

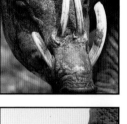

## Bald Eagle (44)

**LENGTH** 34 to 43 inches,
6- to 8-foot wingspan
**GROUP** Bird
**DIET** Carnivore

## Banana Slug (129)

**LENGTH** 6 to 10 inches
**GROUP** Mollusk
**DIET** Herbivore

## Barn Owl (90)

**LENGTH** 12 to 16 inches,
4-foot wingspan
**GROUP** Bird
**DIET** Carnivore

## Beaver (115)

**LENGTH** 23 to 39 inches
**GROUP** Mammal
**DIET** Herbivore

## Bighorn Sheep (84)

**LENGTH** 5 to 6 feet
**GROUP** Mammal
**DIET** Herbivore

## Bison (58)

**LENGTH** 7 to 11.5 feet
**GROUP** Mammal
**DIET** Herbivore

## Black Bear (135)

**LENGTH** 5 to 6 feet
**GROUP** Mammal
**DIET** Omnivore

## Black Mamba (141)

**LENGTH** Up to 14 feet
**GROUP** Reptile
**DIET** Carnivore

## Blobfish (75)

**LENGTH** 11 inches
**GROUP** Fish
**DIET** Carnivore

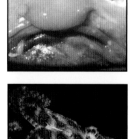

## Blue-Ringed Octopus (140)

**LENGTH** 4.5 to 5 inches
**GROUP** Mollusk
**DIET** Carnivore

# Index

## Blue Whale (160)

**LENGTH** 82 to 105 feet
**GROUP** Mammal
**DIET** Carnivore

## Bobcat (153)

**LENGTH** 26 to 41 inches
**GROUP** Mammal
**DIET** Carnivore

## Bobolink (89)

**LENGTH** 6.3 to 7.1 inches,
11.5-inch wingspan
**GROUP** Bird
**DIET** Omnivore

## Brown Hare (111)

**LENGTH** 20 to 24 inches
**GROUP** Mammal
**DIET** Herbivore

## Brown Recluse Spider (142)

**LENGTH** 0.25 to 0.8 inches
**GROUP** Arthropod
**DIET** Carnivore

## Burmese Python (69)

**LENGTH** 25 to 30 feet
**GROUP** Reptile
**DIET** Carnivore

## Bush Viper (76)

**LENGTH** 22 to 28 inches
**GROUP** Reptile
**DIET** Carnivore

## Cactus Ferruginous Pygmy-Owl (151)

**LENGTH** 6.5 to 7 inches,
14.5- to 16-inch wingspan
**GROUP** Bird
**DIET** Carnivore

## Cactus Wren (153)

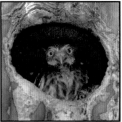

**LENGTH** 7 to 9 inches,
8- to 12-inch wingspan
**GROUP** Bird
**DIET** Omnivore

## Caecilian (131)

**LENGTH** 3.5 inches to 5 feet
**GROUP** Amphibian
**DIET** Carnivore

## Camel (151)

**HEIGHT** 7 feet
**GROUP** Mammal
**DIET** Herbivore

## Canadian Goose (86)

**LENGTH** 30 to 43 inches,
50- to 67-inch wingspan
**GROUP** Bird
**DIET** Herbivore

## Capybara (118)

**LENGTH** 38 to 50 inches
**GROUP** Mammal
**DIET** Herbivore

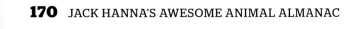

## Caribou (15)

**LENGTH** 5 to 7 feet
**GROUP** Mammal
**DIET** Herbivore

## Cassowary (100)

**LENGTH** 38 to 67 inches
**GROUP** Bird
**DIET** Omnivore

## Cat (79)

**LENGTH** 18 inches
**GROUP** Mammal
**DIET** Carnivore

## Caterpillar (167)

**LENGTH** 1 to 2 inches
**GROUP** Arthropod
**DIET** Herbivore

## Cheetah (113)

**LENGTH** 3.5 to 4.5 feet
**GROUP** Mammal
**DIET** Carnivore

## Chicken (34)

**LENGTH** 16 to 24 inches,
18- to 24-inch wingspan
**GROUP** Bird
**DIET** Omnivore

## Chimpanzee (20)

**HEIGHT** 4 to 5.5 feet
**GROUP** Mammal
**DIET** Omnivore

## Chinchilla (114)

**LENGTH** 9 to 15 inches
**GROUP** Mammal
**DIET** Omnivore

## Chipmunk (96)

**LENGTH** 4 to 7 inches
**GROUP** Mammal
**DIET** Omnivore

## Coati (100)

**LENGTH** 13 to 24 inches
**GROUP** Mammal
**DIET** Omnivore

## Cockroach (162)

**LENGTH** 2 inches
**GROUP** Arthropod
**DIET** Omnivore

## Common Merganser (71)

**LENGTH** 23 to 28 inches,
31- to 38-inch wingspan
**GROUP** Bird
**DIET** Carnivore

## Cone Snail (139)

**LENGTH** 4 to 6 inches
**GROUP** Mollusk
**DIET** Carnivore

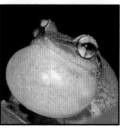

## Coqui Frog (159)

**LENGTH** 1 to 2 inches
**GROUP** Amphibian
**DIET** Carnivore

# Index

### Coral (131)
**LENGTH** 0.25 to 12 inches
**GROUP** Coelenterate
**DIET** Carnivore

### Degu (116)
**LENGTH** 10 to 12 inches
**GROUP** Mammal
**DIET** Herbivore

### Cownose Ray (85)
**LENGTH** Up to 3.5 feet
**GROUP** Fish
**DIET** Carnivore

### Desert Locust (61)
**LENGTH** 0.5 to 3 inches
**GROUP** Arthropod
**DIET** Herbivore

### Cricket (165)
**LENGTH** 0.12 to 2 inches
**GROUP** Arthropod
**DIET** Omnivore

### Desert Tortoise (154)
**LENGTH** 6 to 14 inches
**GROUP** Reptile
**DIET** Herbivore

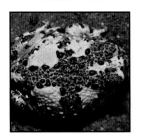

### Crucifix Toad (105)
**LENGTH** 1.7 to 2.5 inches
**GROUP** Amphibian
**DIET** Carnivore

### Dog (31)
**LENGTH** 6 to 48 inches
**GROUP** Mammal
**DIET** Carnivore

### Cuttlefish (129)
**LENGTH** 6 to 20 inches
**GROUP** Mollusk
**DIET** Carnivore

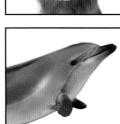

### Dolphin (53)
**LENGTH** 10 to 14 feet
**GROUP** Mammal
**DIET** Carnivore

### Donkey (32)
**LENGTH** 30 to 62 inches
**GROUP** Mammal
**DIET** Herbivore

**D**

### Dalmatian (121)
**LENGTH** 19 to 23 inches
**GROUP** Mammal
**DIET** Omnivore

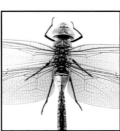

### Dragonfly (47)
**LENGTH** 1 to 4 inches
**GROUP** Arthropod
**DIET** Carnivore

## Dugong (37)

**LENGTH** 8 to 10 feet
**GROUP** Mammal
**DIET** Herbivore

## Dung Beetle (64)

**LENGTH** 0.2 to 2.4 inches
**GROUP** Arthropod
**DIET** Omnivore

# E

## Echidna (80)

**LENGTH** 12 to 18 inches
**GROUP** Mammal
**DIET** Carnivore

## Elephant (51)

**HEIGHT** 8 to 13 feet
**GROUP** Mammal
**DIET** Herbivore

## Emperor Penguin (149)

**LENGTH** 45 inches,
30- to 35-inch wingspan
**GROUP** Bird
**DIET** Carnivore

## Erigone Spider (46)

**LENGTH** 0.5 to 1 inch
**GROUP** Arthropod
**DIET** Carnivore

# F

## Fennec Fox (93)

**LENGTH** 9.5 to 16 inches
**GROUP** Mammal
**DIET** Omnivore

## Ferret (30)

**LENGTH** 15 to 20 inches
**GROUP** Mammal
**DIET** Carnivore

## Flamingo (147)

**LENGTH** 36 to 50 inches,
5-foot wingspan
**GROUP** Bird
**DIET** Omnivore

## Flat-Headed Cat (145)

**LENGTH** 13 to 19.5 inches
**GROUP** Mammal
**DIET** Carnivore

## Flea (62)

**LENGTH** 0.05 to 0.125 inches
**GROUP** Arthropod
**DIET** Carnivore

## Flying Frog (45)

**LENGTH** 4 inches
**GROUP** Amphibian
**DIET** Carnivore

# Index

## Fossa (102)
**LENGTH** 23.5 to 30 inches
**GROUP** Mammal
**DIET** Carnivore

## Frigatebird (111)
**LENGTH** 2 to 3 feet,
5- to 8-foot wingspan
**GROUP** Bird
**DIET** Carnivore

## Gazelle (55)
**HEIGHT** 20 to 43 inches
**GROUP** Mammal
**DIET** Herbivore

## Gemsbok (59)
**HEIGHT** 47 inches
**GROUP** Mammal
**DIET** Herbivore

## Giant Isopod (72)
**LENGTH** 7.5 to 14.2 inches
**GROUP** Arthropod
**DIET** Carnivore

## Giant Panda (136)
**LENGTH** 4 to 5 feet
**GROUP** Mammal
**DIET** Carnivore

## Giant Squid (127)
**LENGTH** 33 feet
**GROUP** Mollusk
**DIET** Carnivore

## Gibbon (18)
**LENGTH** 17 to 25 inches
**GROUP** Mammal
**DIET** Omnivore

## Gila Monster (152)
**LENGTH** 20 inches
**GROUP** Reptile
**DIET** Carnivore

## Giraffe (57)
**LENGTH** 14 to 19 feet
**GROUP** Mammal
**DIET** Herbivore

## Goat (30)
**HEIGHT** 3.5 feet
**GROUP** Mammal
**DIET** Herbivore

## Gobi Bear (134)
**LENGTH** 5 feet
**GROUP** Mammal
**DIET** Omnivore

## Gorilla (49)
**LENGTH** 4 to 6 feet
**GROUP** Mammal
**DIET** Omnivore

## Grasshopper Mouse (107)

**LENGTH** 6.5 inches
**GROUP** Mammal
**DIET** Omnivore

## Gray Wolf (158)

**LENGTH** 36 to 63 inches
**GROUP** Mammal
**DIET** Carnivore

## Great White Shark (67)

**LENGTH** 15 to 20 feet
**GROUP** Fish
**DIET** Carnivore

## Green Basilisk Lizard (105)

**LENGTH** 2 to 2.5 feet
**GROUP** Reptile
**DIET** Omnivore

## Green Grocer Cicada (156)

**LENGTH** 0.75 to 2.25 inches
**GROUP** Arthropod
**DIET** Herbivore

## Grizzly Bear (132)

**LENGTH** 5 to 8 feet
**GROUP** Mammal
**DIET** Omnivore

## Groundhog (117)

**LENGTH** 18 to 24 inches
**GROUP** Mammal
**DIET** Herbivore

## Hamster (80)

**LENGTH** 1.8 to 4 inches
**GROUP** Mammal
**DIET** Herbivore

## Harp Seal (15)

**LENGTH** 5.25 to 6.25 feet
**GROUP** Mammal
**DIET** Carnivore

## Hawk Moth (27)

**LENGTH** 3 inches,
4- to 5-inch wingspan
**GROUP** Arthropod
**DIET** Herbivore

## Hippopotamus (95)

**LENGTH** 9.5 to 14 feet
**GROUP** Mammal
**DIET** Herbivore

## Honeybee (166)

**LENGTH** 0.4 to 0.6 inches,
1-inch wingspan
**GROUP** Arthropod
**DIET** Herbivore

## Horse (55)

**HEIGHT** 30 to 69 inches
**GROUP** Mammal
**DIET** Herbivore

# Index

## Horsefly (110)
**LENGTH** 1.6 inches,
2.4-inch wingspan
**GROUP** Arthropod
**DIET** Omnivore

## Howler Monkey (157)
**LENGTH** 22 to 36 inches
**GROUP** Mammal
**DIET** Omnivore

## Hummingbird (43)
**LENGTH** 3 to 4 inches,
3-inch wingspan
**GROUP** Bird
**DIET** Omnivore

## Hyena (51)
**LENGTH** 34 to 59 inches
**GROUP** Mammal
**DIET** Omnivore

**I**

## Iberian Ribbed Newt (142)
**LENGTH** 8 to 9 inches
**GROUP** Reptile
**DIET** Carnivore

## Indian Flying Fox (91)
**LENGTH** 9 inches,
4- to 5-foot wingspan
**GROUP** Mammal
**DIET** Herbivore

## Indian Red Scorpion (143)
**LENGTH** 2 to 3.5 inches
**GROUP** Arthropod
**DIET** Carnivore

**J**

## Jaguar (102)
**LENGTH** 5 to 6 feet
**GROUP** Mammal
**DIET** Carnivore

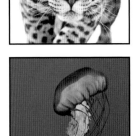

## Jellyfish (126)
**LENGTH** 10 feet
**GROUP** Coelenterate
**DIET** Carnivore

## Jerboa (94)
**LENGTH** 2 to 6 inches
**GROUP** Mammal
**DIET** Omnivore

**K**

## Kangaroo (22)
**HEIGHT** 6 feet
**GROUP** Mammal
**DIET** Herbivore

## Killifish (167)

**LENGTH** 2 to 3.5 inches
**GROUP** Fish
**DIET** Carnivore

## Kinkajou (94)

**LENGTH** 17 to 22 inches
**GROUP** Mammal
**DIET** Omnivore

## Koala (79)

**LENGTH** 2 to 3 feet
**GROUP** Mammal
**DIET** Herbivore

## Kodiak Bear (137)

**LENGTH** 8 feet
**GROUP** Mammal
**DIET** Omnivore

## Ladybug (104)

**LENGTH** 0.3 to 0.4 inches
**GROUP** Arthropod
**DIET** Omnivore

## Lamprey (76)

**LENGTH** 6 to 40 inches
**GROUP** Fish
**DIET** Carnivore

## Leafy Sea Dragon (24)

**LENGTH** up to 13.8 inches
**GROUP** Fish
**DIET** Carnivore

## Leopard (28)

**LENGTH** 4.25 to 6.25 feet
**GROUP** Mammal
**DIET** Carnivore

## Lightning Bug (60)

**LENGTH** 1 inch
**GROUP** Arthropod
**DIET** Omnivore

## Lion (159)

**LENGTH** 4.5 to 6.5 feet
**GROUP** Mammal
**DIET** Carnivore

## Llama (57)

**HEIGHT** 47 inches
**GROUP** Mammal
**DIET** Herbivore

## Lobster (93)

**LENGTH** Up to 3.25 feet
**GROUP** Mollusk
**DIET** Omnivore

## Long-Nosed Weevil (65)

**LENGTH** 0.25 inches
**GROUP** Arthropod
**DIET** Herbivore

# Index

## Long-Tailed Weasel (107)

**LENGTH** 11 to 16.5 inches
**GROUP** Mammal
**DIET** Carnivore

# M

## Manatee (88)

**LENGTH** 8 to 13 feet
**GROUP** Mammal
**DIET** Herbivore

## Maned Wolf (96)

**LENGTH** 4 feet
**GROUP** Mammal
**DIET** Omnivore

## Mara (118)

**LENGTH** 27 to 29 inches
**GROUP** Mammal
**DIET** Herbivore

## Markhor (58)

**LENGTH** 51 to 72 inches
**GROUP** Mammal
**DIET** Herbivore

## Mastiff (70)

**LENGTH** 2.5 feet
**GROUP** Mammal
**DIET** Carnivore

## Meerkat (52)

**LENGTH** 9.75 to 11.75 inches
**GROUP** Mammal
**DIET** Omnivore

## Mexican Free-Tailed Bat (108)

**LENGTH** 3.7 inches, 11-inch wingspan
**GROUP** Mammal
**DIET** Carnivore

## Mimic Octopus (24)

**LENGTH** 2 feet
**GROUP** Mollusk
**DIET** Carnivore

## Monarch Butterfly (88)

**LENGTH** Up to 0.23 inches,
3.7- to 4.1-inch wingspan
**GROUP** Arthropod
**DIET** Herbivore

## Mongoose (41)

**LENGTH** 7 to 25 inches
**GROUP** Mammal
**DIET** Carnivore

## Moose (87)

**LENGTH** 5 to 6.5 feet
**GROUP** Mammal
**DIET** Herbivore

## Mud Crab (165)

**LENGTH** 6 to 9.5 inches
**GROUP** Arthropod
**DIET** Omnivore

## Musk Deer (66)

**LENGTH** 19 to 28 inches
**GROUP** Mammal
**DIET** Herbivore

## Musk Ox (13)

**LENGTH** 4 to 5 feet
**GROUP** Mammal
**DIET** Herbivore

## Muskrat (146)

**LENGTH** 16 to 25 inches
**GROUP** Mammal
**DIET** Omnivore

# N

## Naked Mole Rat (74)

**LENGTH** 3 to 13 inches
**GROUP** Mammal
**DIET** Herbivore

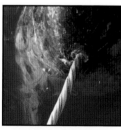

## Narwhal (17)

**LENGTH** 13 to 20 feet
**GROUP** Mammal
**DIET** Carnivore

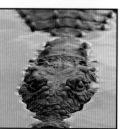

## Nile Crocodile (103)

**LENGTH** 16 feet
**GROUP** Reptile
**DIET** Carnivore

## North American River Otter (146)

**LENGTH** 21 to 32 inches
**GROUP** Mammal
**DIET** Carnivore

## Northern Flying Squirrel (44)

**LENGTH** 10 to 12 inches
**GROUP** Mammal
**DIET** Omnivore

# O

## Ocelot (120)

**LENGTH** 28 to 35 inches
**GROUP** Mammal
**DIET** Carnivore

## Olm Salamander (72)

**LENGTH** 8 to 12 inches
**GROUP** Amphibian
**DIET** Carnivore

## Opossum (83)

**LENGTH** 2.5 feet
**GROUP** Mammal
**DIET** Omnivore

## Orangutan (36)

**LENGTH** 4 to 5 feet
**GROUP** Mammal
**DIET** Omnivore

# Index

## Orca (17)
**LENGTH** 23 to 32 feet
**GROUP** Mammal
**DIET** Carnivore

## Ostrich (19)
**LENGTH** 7 to 9 feet, 6.6-foot wingspan
**GROUP** Bird
**DIET** Omnivore

## Owl Monkey (83)
**LENGTH** 13 inches
**GROUP** Mammal
**DIET** Omnivore

## Paca (117)
**LENGTH** 24 to 31 inches
**GROUP** Mammal
**DIET** Herbivore

## Pangolin (40)
**LENGTH** 1.5 to 3 feet
**GROUP** Mammal
**DIET** Carnivore

## Peacock (23)
**LENGTH** 34 to 42 inches,
47- to 118-inch wingspan
**GROUP** Bird
**DIET** Omnivore

## Peregrine Falcon (109)
**LENGTH** 14 to 19 inches,
39- to 43-inch wingspan
**GROUP** Bird
**DIET** Carnivore

## Pietrain Pig (123)
**LENGTH** 3 to 4.5 feet
**GROUP** Mammal
**DIET** Omnivore

## Pigeon (33)
**LENGTH** 11 to 14 inches,
20- to 26-inch wingspan
**GROUP** Bird
**DIET** Omnivore

## Pileated (98) Woodpecker
**LENGTH** 16 to 19 inches,
26- to 30-inch wingspan
**GROUP** Bird
**DIET** Omnivore

## Pill Bug (163)
**LENGTH** 0.75 inches
**GROUP** Arthropod
**DIET** Herbivore

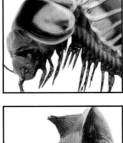

## Piranha (101)
**LENGTH** 10 to 14 inches
**GROUP** Fish
**DIET** Omnivore

## Platypus (148)
**LENGTH** 15 inches
**GROUP** Mammal
**DIET** Carnivore

## Polar Bear
(134)

**LENGTH** 7.25 to 8 feet
**GROUP** Mammal
**DIET** Carnivore

## Porcupine (119)

**LENGTH** 2 to 3 feet
**GROUP** Mammal
**DIET** Herbivore

## Prairie Dog (160)

**LENGTH** 12 to 15 inches
**GROUP** Mammal
**DIET** Herbivore

## Praying Mantis (61)

**LENGTH** 2 to 5 inches
**GROUP** Arthropod
**DIET** Carnivore

## Pronghorn (154)

**LENGTH** 3.25 to 5 feet
**GROUP** Mammal
**DIET** Herbivore

# Q

## Quokka (18)

**LENGTH** 15 to 21 inches
**GROUP** Mammal
**DIET** Herbivore

# R

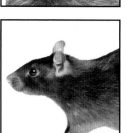

## Raccoon (97)

**LENGTH** 2 to 3 feet
**GROUP** Mammal
**DIET** Omnivore

## Rat (114)

**LENGTH** 6.7 to 8.3 inches
**GROUP** Mammal
**DIET** Omnivore

## Red-Lipped Batfish (74)

**LENGTH** 15 to 16 inches
**GROUP** Fish
**DIET** Carnivore

## Red Squirrel (157)

**LENGTH** 5 to 36 inches
**GROUP** Mammal
**DIET** Omnivore

## Rhesus Macaque (50)

**LENGTH** 17.75 to 25 inches
**GROUP** Mammal
**DIET** Omnivore

## Ribbon Seal (14)

**LENGTH** 62 inches
**GROUP** Mammal
**DIET** Carnivore

# Index

### Ring-Tailed Lemur (81)

**LENGTH** 17.75 inches
**GROUP** Mammal
**DIET** Herbivore

### Rüppell's Vulture (46)

**LENGTH** 33 to 41 inches,
7.5- to 8.5-foot wingspan
**GROUP** Bird
**DIET** Carnivore

## S

### Sailfish (108)

**LENGTH** 5.5 to 11 feet
**GROUP** Fish
**DIET** Carnivore

### Salmon (86)

**LENGTH** 19 to 47 inches
**GROUP** Fish
**DIET** Omnivore

### Saola (40)

**LENGTH** 3 to 4 feet
**GROUP** Mammal
**DIET** Herbivore

### Scarlet Kingsnake (26)

**LENGTH** 14 to 20 inches
**GROUP** Reptile
**DIET** Carnivore

### Screech Owl (25)

**LENGTH** 5 to 6.3 inches,
15-inch wingspan
**GROUP** Bird
**DIET** Carnivore

### Sea Anemone (128)

**LENGTH** 0.5 inch to 6 foot diameter
**GROUP** Coelenterate
**DIET** Carnivore

### Sea Turtle (39)

**LENGTH** 3 to 5 feet
**GROUP** Reptile
**DIET** Herbivore

### Seahorse (73)

**LENGTH** 0.6 to 14 inches
**GROUP** Fish
**DIET** Carnivore

### Skunk (99)

**LENGTH** 5 to 15 inches
**GROUP** Mammal
**DIET** Omnivore

### Sloth (82)

**LENGTH** 2 to 2.5 feet
**GROUP** Mammal
**DIET** Herbivore

### Sloth Bear (137)

**LENGTH** 5 to 6 feet
**GROUP** Mammal
**DIET** Omnivore

## Slow Loris (141)

**LENGTH** 7 to 15 inches
**GROUP** Mammal
**DIET** Omnivore

## Spot-Billed Duck (145)

**LENGTH** 23.5 to 25.5 inches,
31.5- to 35.5-inch wingspan
**GROUP** Bird
**DIET** Omnivore

## Snail (127)

**LENGTH** 1 to 12 inches
**GROUP** Mollusk
**DIET** Herbivore

## Spotted Bush Snake (124)

**LENGTH** 2 to 3 feet
**GROUP** Reptile
**DIET** Carnivore

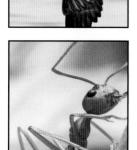

## Sooty Shearwater (84)

**LENGTH** 15 to 20 inches,
3- to 3.5-foot wingspan
**GROUP** Bird
**DIET** Carnivore

## Spotted Moray Eel (125)

**LENGTH** 6.5 feet
**GROUP** Fish
**DIET** Carnivore

## South American Fire Ant (163)

**LENGTH** 0.06 to 0.2 inches
**GROUP** Arthropod
**DIET** Omnivore

## Spotted Trunkfish (123)

**LENGTH** 6 to 12 inches
**GROUP** Fish
**DIET** Omnivore

## Spectacled Bear (133)

**LENGTH** 5 to 6 feet
**GROUP** Mammal
**DIET** Omnivore

## Spotted Turtle (125)

**LENGTH** 5.3 inches
**GROUP** Reptile
**DIET** Omnivore

## Spider Monkey (21)

**LENGTH** 15 to 26 inches
**GROUP** Mammal
**DIET** Omnivore

## Springbok (112)

**LENGTH** 4 to 4.5 feet
**GROUP** Mammal
**DIET** Herbivore

## Spine-Tailed Swift (42)

**LENGTH** 7.8 inches,
14-inch wingspan
**GROUP** Bird
**DIET** Carnivore

## Springhare (21)

**LENGTH** 14 to 19 inches
**GROUP** Mammal
**DIET** Omnivore

# Index

### Star-Nosed Mole (130)
**LENGTH** 6 to 8 inches
**GROUP** Mammal
**DIET** Carnivore

### Stink Bug (63)
**LENGTH** 0.7 inches
**GROUP** Arthropod
**DIET** Omnivore

### Stoat (12)
**LENGTH** 6 to 12 inches
**GROUP** Mammal
**DIET** Carnivore

### Stonefish (138)
**LENGTH** 12 to 16 inches
**GROUP** Fish
**DIET** Carnivore

### Sugar Glider (43)
**LENGTH** 5 to 7 inches
**GROUP** Mammal
**DIET** Omnivore

### Sumatran Rhino (37)
**LENGTH** 8 to 10 feet
**GROUP** Mammal
**DIET** Herbivore

### Sun Bear (133)
**LENGTH** 4 to 5 feet
**GROUP** Mammal
**DIET** Omnivore

### Sun Conure (52)
**LENGTH** 1 foot, 18-inch wingspan
**GROUP** Bird
**DIET** Omnivore

### Swordfish (113)
**LENGTH** 6 to 14 feet
**GROUP** Fish
**DIET** Carnivore

# T

### Tapir (56)
**HEIGHT** 29 to 42 inches
**GROUP** Mammal
**DIET** Herbivore

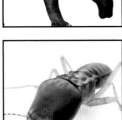

### Termite (62)
**LENGTH** 0.25 to 0.5 inches
**GROUP** Arthropod
**DIET** Herbivore

### Thorn Bug (28)
**LENGTH** 0.5 inches
**GROUP** Arthropod
**DIET** Herbivore

### Thorny Devil (150)
**LENGTH** 6 to 8 inches
**GROUP** Reptile
**DIET** Omnivore

### Tiger (66)

**LENGTH** 5 to 6 feet
**GROUP** Mammal
**DIET** Carnivore

### Trapdoor Spider (106)

**LENGTH** 1 to 1.5 inches
**GROUP** Arthropod
**DIET** Carnivore

### Trumpeter Swan (144)

**LENGTH** 5.5 feet, 10-foot wingspan
**GROUP** Bird
**DIET** Herbivore

# V

### Vampire Bat (49)

**LENGTH** 3.5 inches, 7-inch wingspan
**GROUP** Mammal
**DIET** Carnivore

### Velvet Worm (49)

**LENGTH** 0.8 to 8 inches
**GROUP** Worm
**DIET** Carnivore

### Viceroy Butterfly (29)

**LENGTH** 2.5 to 3.5-inch wingspan
**GROUP** Arthropod
**DIET** Herbivore

# W

### Walking Stick (27)

**LENGTH** 1 to 12 inches long
**GROUP** Arthropod
**DIET** Herbivore

### Walrus (13)

**LENGTH** 7 to 11.5 feet
**GROUP** Mammal
**DIET** Carnivore

### Wasp (139)

**LENGTH** Up to 1.5 inches
**GROUP** Arthropod
**DIET** Omnivore

### Water Buffalo (33)

**LENGTH** 8 to 9 feet
**GROUP** Mammal
**DIET** Herbivore

### Whale Shark (121)

**LENGTH** 18 to 33 feet
**GROUP** Fish
**DIET** Carnivore

### Wood Frog (164)

**LENGTH** 1.4 to 3.5 inches
**GROUP** Amphibian
**DIET** Omnivore

# Index

## Woolly Monkey (99)
**LENGTH** 20 to 24 inches
**GROUP** Mammal
**DIET** Omnivore

**Y**

## Yak (34)
**LENGTH** 8.2 to 11 feet
**GROUP** Mammal
**DIET** Herbivore

## Yeti Crab (77)
**LENGTH** 6 inches
**GROUP** Mollusk
**DIET** Carnivore

**Z**

## Zebra (54)
**HEIGHT** 3.5 to 5 feet
**GROUP** Mammal
**DIET** Herbivore

What a wild list of animals!

**Media Lab Books**
**For inquiries, call 646-838-6637**

Copyright 2017 Topix Media Lab

Published by Topix Media Lab
14 Wall Street, Suite 4B
New York, NY 10005

Printed in China

ISBN-10: 1-942556-57-8
ISBN-13: 978-1-942556-57-2

**CEO** Tony Romando

**Vice President of Brand Marketing** Joy Bomba
**Director of Finance** Vandana Patel
**Director of Sales and New Markets** Tom Mifsud
**Manufacturing Director** Nancy Puskuldjian
**Financial Analyst** Matthew Quinn
**Brand Marketing Assistant** Taylor Hamilton

**Editor-in-Chief** Jeff Ashworth
**Creative Director** Steven Charny
**Photo Director** Dave Weiss
**Managing Editor** Courtney Kerrigan
**Senior Editors** Tim Baker, James Ellis

**Content Editor** Kaytie Norman
**Content Designer** Michelle Lock
**Content Photo Editor** Catherine Armanasco
**Art Director** Susan Dazzo
**Assistant Managing Editor** Holland Baker
**Designer** Danielle Santucci
**Assistant Editors** Trevor Courneen, Alicia Kort
**Editorial Assistant** Isabella Torchia

**Co-Founders** Bob Lee, Tony Romando

# Explore more with Jack Hanna!

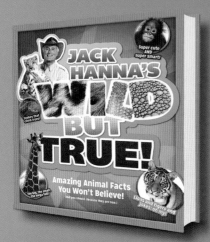

ISBN-10: 1942556209

## JACK HANNA'S WILD BUT TRUE

Did you know snakes can climb trees? Or that a group of ferrets is called a business? Check out tons of wild but true facts just like these in this 175-page book full of colorful photos!

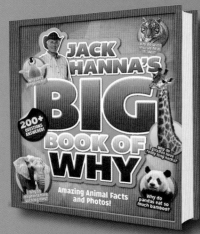

ISBN-10: 1942556020

## JACK HANNA'S BIG BOOK OF WHY

Why do camels spit? Why aren't bald eagles bald? Why do elephants have such big ears? Find out the answers to these and more than 200 other animal questions in this entertaining and educational photo-filled book!

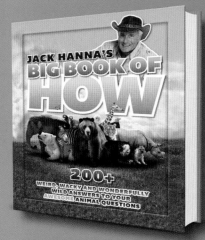

ISBN-10: 1942556284

## JACK HANNA'S BIG BOOK OF HOW

How do jellyfish swim? How do bees make their hives? Discover the answers to 200+ weird, wacky and wonderful questions in this incredible fact-filled book!

**AVAILABLE WHEREVER BOOKS ARE SOLD**

# TAKE A TRIP AROUND THE GLOBE WITH JACK HANNA!

Join nearly **3 MILLION HOUSEHOLDS** watching Jungle Jack Hanna's exciting wildlife adventures from the comfort of your living room each weekend!

Visit WildCountdown.com or tune into ABC stations this Saturday morning to catch the adventure!

Visit jhitw.com or check your local listings for show times.

presented by

**Now available on-demand!**

Search "Jack Hanna" on   and

# ADOPT

ADOPT AN ANIMAL FOR YOURSELF
OR A LOVED ONE AT:

GIVE.COLUMBUSZOO.ORG/ADOPT
ADOPT@COLUMBUSZOO.ORG
614.724.3497

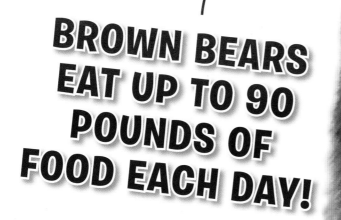

# Take care, brown bear!

**BROWN BEARS EAT UP TO 90 POUNDS OF FOOD EACH DAY!**